The Not-Very-Persecuted Church

The Not-Very-Persecuted Church

Paul at the Intersection of Church and Culture

Laura J. Hunt

with foreword by
J. Brian Tucker,

RESOURCE *Publications* · Eugene, Oregon

THE NOT-VERY-PERSECUTED CHURCH
Paul at the Intersection of Church and Culture

Resource Publications
An Imprint of Wipf and Stock Publishers
199 W. 8th Ave., Suite 3
Eugene, OR 97401

www.wipfandstock.com

ISBN 13: 978-1-61097-606-0

Manufactured in the U.S.A.

To Doug, who always believes I can

Contents

Foreword

THE CORINTHIAN CHRIST-FOLLOWERS ARE often berated by pastors and sometimes by scholars for 'just not getting it.' How could this community have developed so many glaring weaknesses in such a short period? While this group undoubtedly had more than their share of problems, outside persecution was not one of them. Scholars have come to recognize that in comparison to those in Thessalonica and Philippi, the Christ-movement in Corinth did not suffer persecution from the imperial authorities or their provincial collaborators. This unique set of circumstances may have inadvertently contributed to the internal problems among the Christ-followers in Corinth.

The implicit message of acceptance by the authorities allowed for peaceful co-existence between the local governing elites and those in the Christ-movement. Add to this Paul's rule that each should stay in the social situation in which each one was called (1 Cor 7:17–24), and you have a social matrix ripe for effective mission but also maximum confusion. Paul sees the continuation of existing social identities as a means of mission, but the Corinthians needed clarification about the way local expressions of their Roman identity were to be configured within the Christ-movement (1 Cor 5:9–10), especially since some were evidently using this freedom in a way that Paul viewed with concern (1 Cor 6:12; 10:23). Paul's letters serve as pastoral formation from afar as he seeks to ensure that the in-Christ social identity would maintain its salience in the various cultural interchanges in Corinth (1 Cor 10:32; 12:13). The realization that Paul seeks to reprioritize existing social identities, rather than to call for their obliteration, is a key finding among a group of scholars who may be loosely described as beyond the new perspective on Paul. Within this group, Paul is seen to be thoroughly embedded in

Judaism, mainly concerned with the imperial hegemony of the Roman Empire, and fighting for the continuation of both Jewish and gentile social identities in Christ.

The discussion and reconsideration of Paul's approach to identity formation has occurred, until recently, primarily in Romans and Galatians, which is to be expected. Interestingly, little attention has been paid to 1 Corinthians because it is assumed that there is little interest in ethnic identity in that letter. While the issues are different, the focus only on ethnic identity has led to comparatively little attention being paid to the broader area of social identity, of which ethnic identity is a small but important part. First Corinthians is one of Paul's most expansive expressions of the challenges associated with social identity and group membership, especially when there is not an external threat to the group's existence.

It is this situation that Laura Hunt sets out to address in *The Not-Very-Persecuted Church*. She takes on the task of seeing what a particularistic approach to social identity, when applied to 1 Corinthians 1—4, with the realization that there was a lack of official persecution in this Roman colony, tells us about the formation of Christ-movement identity and mission. She takes seriously God's call for Christ-followers to live in community and uncovers the processes of identity formation that, when taken into consideration, increase the likelihood of unity and mission effectiveness (1 Cor 9:19–23). The church today oftentimes shows too much evidence of internal conflict with groups staking out their side of theological debates and talking past other Christians, and invariably forgetting that all those in Christ belong to the same Father (1 Cor 3:16, 23). What is often missed is that a theological problem may really be an identity problem, as William S. Campbell points out: "*identity precedes theology and . . . in fact theological constructions emerge to solve the problem of identity rather than create it.*"[1] First Corinthians 1—4 is particularly helpful in this situation, in that the problems in Corinth were not theological, per se, but were identity related. Thinking about identity and reading the Bible through the lens of identity provides a focus for the type of community God desires and increases the likelihood that the church will stay on mission.

Throughout this book you will be introduced to the concept of social identity. You'll meet a Paul whose Jewishness comes to the fore, and

---

1. Campbell, *Christian Identity*, 52. Emphasis original.

the Corinthians will be described in their first century Roman context. These chapters will combine to provide a fresh perspective for reading the text. The chapters that follow, which are full of exegetical nuggets and stories to keep your attention, provide a convincing reading of 1 Corinthians 1—4 that shows the Corinthian Christ-followers to be just like us, individuals who find their identity in the groups we are part of *and* in Christ. The challenge for us, like them, is how to navigate the balance between our ever-changing social situations so that our in-Christ identity remains salient and we are able to maintain our outward, mission focus while enjoying the benefits of the culture that is around us—under the Lordship of Christ.

This is but the tip of Laura Hunt's concern in this book. It is a work that makes sometimes arcane and detailed arguments accessible. It draws out the social implications of the scriptures in a way that is easily trans-ferable to the lived-out experience of 21st century Christians. This book will provide an important correction to the course steered by others who suggest Christ only wants the world out of the church. It also offers a critical interpretive adjustment with regard to the way church leaders and attendees interpret suffering, or the lack thereof, in their local congrega-tions. I commend it warmly.

J. Brian Tucker
Associate Professor of New Testament,
Moody Theological Seminary

Preface

I WAS RAISED TO believe in the god of education. "Go to school, learn, and you will accomplish great things." My dad encouraged me to be anything I wanted to be . . . but you had to be stupid to be a Christian.

When I was seventeen, however, I met Jesus. I couldn't *not* believe in someone so real. I rebelled against my family by becoming an evangelical Christian. I married my high school sweetheart and became a mom, eventually a home schooling mom, to five children. I enjoyed twenty-five years of ups and downs, living a life which revolved around marriage, family, and church.

Then God called me back to school. My husband supported me, and my kids cheered for me as I finished my Bachelor's degree and got a Master's in Theological Studies. I rediscovered the joy of learning—from a Christian perspective this time. In seminary, I added loving the Lord with all my mind to loving him with all my heart, soul, and strength. I wanted to share these new academic topics with others.

When Dr. J. Brian Tucker asked me to edit the PhD thesis that eventually turned into his book *You Belong to Christ*, I really enjoyed the challenge of understanding his ideas. And even when I put the papers down, I continued to see the concepts he described in the world around me. I realized how often I use language to define ingroups and outgroups. I recognized models and types and watched group identities shift up and down ladders—others' and my own. I saw the assumptions of our culture influencing assumptions in the church. I began to question who I was in Christ, how my cultural experiences had shaped me, how the groups I belong to define who I am. *You Belong to Christ* explains those concepts beautifully—in academic language. This book is my attempt to translate that information and share that journey with you.

The book progresses through identity-driven questions to some answers from 1 Corinthians 1—4. The first two chapters explain some of the ways that people act in groups, especially when they do not feel pressure from the outside. The next two chapters present Paul and the people of Corinth in their historical context. Chapters 5–9 analyze the first four chapters of 1 Corinthians using the information on group identity given in the first half of the book. The final chapter shows the way Paul's words to the Corinthians can reshape our identity today.

Since this book is based on academic writing but not intended for scholarly reading, I have only included a limited number of footnotes. Chapter 2 draws from the work of Henri Tajfel and John Turner. For an introduction to social identity theory, start with the books by Hogg and Jenkins included in the bibliography.

If you are familiar with recent scholarship on Paul, you will notice some assumptions in this book that follow the new perspective, especially those that highlight Paul's Jewish background. Further than that, though, and following scholars sometimes called beyond the new perspective, I assume a continuing place for both Paul's Jewish identity and the gentile identity of non-Jewish followers of Christ. For more in-depth discussions of these positions, interested readers should start with Tucker's book, *You Belong to Christ*, and follow the footnotes for references to the scholarly debates. Although this work is based on his, I have interpreted it from my own perspective so the opinions and any mistakes are solely my own.

I hope you like quotes from people living in the first century. I have included them because to me, they feel like peeking through a telescope 2000 years long to make that world become real. However, I have changed British spelling to American for consistency in the translations.

I have included application questions at three or four points in each chapter. They are designed for small group discussion. A leader's guide is available on my website at www.laurajhunt.com. I pray that you have the same experience I did, that as you read and think about Paul's words redefining the identity of the not-very-persecuted followers of Christ in Corinth, you will also hear God's call to us, the Not-Very-Persecuted Church of the twenty-first century, redefining our identity in Christ.

Acknowledgments

I WANT TO THANK Dr. J. Brian Tucker for the insights into his work and for saying yes when I asked if I could write a book based on *You Belong to Christ*. I admire both your scholarship and your pastoral ministry.

Thank you also to the adult Sunday School class that patiently worked through an early draft of this book. Dave, Daryl and Pearl, Michelle, Bethany, Dan and Sharen, your input and encouragement made this book not only better but possible. Thank you, as well, to those of you who shared your stories with me for the chapter beginnings. Valy, Irv, Elliot, Darold, Nadia, John, and Carole, you helped make the book real.

To friends and family who prayed for me and put up with my extended absences, mental or physical—thank you. I am especially grateful to my husband Doug and our three children at home, Kevin, Josh, and Beth, who lived with me lovingly even though my identity as a writer usually took precedence over my identity as housekeeper and cook. Thank you for participating with me in this endeavor.

Many, many thanks to my editors, Kevin Hunt, Marilee Riley, Bev Opal, and Chaley Hunt, as well as so many others who gave their input along the way. Your willingness to tell me what you really thought was priceless.

Finally, grace and peace to all of you as we figure out together what it means to live in Christ.

Laura J. Hunt
August 2011

1

Who Are the Not-Very-Persecuted?

The Lord prompted Valy and his friends to cut the meeting short. "When the last person left the apartment," he said in an interview, "police knocked on the door." As they searched for illegal Christian materials, Valy's wife Elena prayed, "Lord Jesus, please blind them so they won't look in the cabinets." The books and pamphlets hidden there could send them to jail. The police eventually had to leave, apologizing. "I guess there is nothing in this house."

Valy Vaduva led Christian discipleship groups in Communist Romania. Despite brushes with the law such as this, "Christians were getting closer and closer to the Lord, and they were hungry for Bible study and prayer meetings because the persecution made them determined to get closer to the Lord in order to survive spiritually and also in order to be able to witness." Trust in the Lord and in each other was key.

Now Valy lives in the United States but returns regularly for ministry in free Romania. His radio broadcasts cover the country on nine different stations. He sends out flyers by email. He posts advertisements on buildings. But people have many choices of entertainment, and Christians blend with the rest of the culture.

"Before, during the persecution, churches were packed, and even the young generation was eager to pray more and learn more," Valy says. Now he sees greater superficiality.

"God does not prefer one culture versus another, but God would like us to say, 'This is the culture of the church: we practice disciplines, we appreciate prayer and Bible study, we do evangelism and witnessing to the culture around us, because we are Christians.'"

~from an interview with Valy Vaduva,
Upper Room Fellowship Ministry, http://www.urfm.org/

I N THE 1980's, I read the stories of Brother Andrew and his ministry to Christians like Valy behind the Iron Curtain.[1] Today, we hear about the suffering of Chinese house churches. We get prayer updates from the Voice of the Martyrs. We can imagine, although never really know, the way Christians through the centuries have huddled together in secret, praying, studying, praising the God to whom they had given their lives.

This is not, however, our experience. Oh, we may get laughed at sometimes. Some may call us intolerant, irrelevant, old-fashioned, fundamentalist stick-in-the-muds, or even hint that such strongly held faith leads to fascism, terrorism, crusades, and war. But our lives, our families, and for the most part our jobs are not threatened because we identify ourselves as Christians. We are the Not-Very-Persecuted Church.

Sometimes I'm a little jealous of those times and places where communities have experienced persecution. Meeting in the catacombs, dedicated to God to the point of martyrdom, all that danger and adventure seems like a much more romantic, much more passionate expression of love for God than my mortgage payments, grocery shopping, and Sunday school—at least from the safe couch in my living room! I know better, of course. I have experienced other kinds of pain that let me know how silly it is to wish for real persecution. Still, I long for the kind of community I read about, where people trust and depend on each other as they live their lives in total dedication to God.

PERSECUTED FOLLOWERS OF CHRIST

Social science tells us that persecuted people behave in somewhat predictable ways. Members with a low level of commitment, for instance, will leave the community if they can. In the third century in North Africa, some Christians gave in to their Roman persecutors and declared that Caesar, not Jesus, was Lord. Later, when the persecutions were over, they wanted to rejoin the church. The leaders struggled with this. If you can leave and come back with no penalties, what good is perseverance? Then again, should Christians who deny the faith in a moment of weakness really be excluded forever? Didn't Jesus reinstate Peter after his denial (John 21:15–19)? The church eventually resolved these questions, but the point here is that under persecution some people leave.

1. Andrew, et al., *Smuggler*.

On the other hand, people with high levels of commitment connect with the community even more strongly. Their loyalty increases. They may join together and respond to the situation as a group, maybe writing petitions, forming delegations, or, in more extreme circumstances, living underground or going together into exile.

Persecution, then, changes the makeup of a group in two ways. The less committed people leave, and the strongly committed people become even more loyal. This creates a tightly-knit community with a clear, shared focus. Wouldn't we all like to belong to a community like that?

Questions:

1. What stories have you heard about Christians under persecution?

2. Is there anything about those groups that you envy?

3. Have you ever experienced persecution?

4. How could your community pray for Christians who are being persecuted today?

NOT-VERY-PERSECUTED FOLLOWERS OF CHRIST

Persecution is not the reality for everyone, though. Not-very-persecuted Christians also have some predictable behaviors. Let's look at two imaginary people who represent four different tendencies of church members in non-persecuted areas.

Joe just joined Crossroads, the church down the street from his house. He is passionate about his relationship with Jesus, but he doesn't know anyone in this area. He chose this particular denomination so that he could walk to church and save money on gas. His ties to the church community, at least at first, are not strong. He wants his Sunday mornings to run efficiently. What efficient means to him depends on his priorities, and it includes a concern for accuracy, as well. He may value anything from no snow on the sidewalk or no mistakes on the worship slides, to an atmosphere that helps him connect with God and a sermon that challenges him to further Christian growth. He will also be watching to see how accurately the beliefs of this church line up with his own. Each 'Joe' will have a different set of efficiency requirements, and some of them may show his deep faith. But without strong ties to the community, when there is no persecution, he will especially value the efficiency of his own worship experience.

But let's say that the situation changes. One kind of threat that we do experience as members of the Not-Very-Persecuted Church is an attack on us as individuals based on our church affiliation. If one of Joe's coworkers starts teasing him, not for being a Christian but for going to a church that is too charismatic, or too traditional, or too liberal, or too conservative, Joe is likely to respond by distancing himself from Crossroads. He may not quit the church, but he will begin to emphasize to himself and to others the ways that he is different, the ways that he doesn't quite fit in, the ways that he's a Christian but not *really* one of *them*. So when a loosely connected person feels threatened by outsiders, he will probably respond by stepping back a little from the group.

Now Sally has been a member of Crossroads since it started. Her parents belonged to First United, the church that founded Crossroads, and the whole family helped to get the new community started. Sally is proud of how much Crossroads has grown, of the work they are doing in the city and the new podcasts she helps to produce. She wears Crossroads tee shirts on Saturdays and Sunday afternoons and puts flyers for Crossroads events on the bulletin boards at work. When a person with strong ties to a group does not feel persecuted, she often makes decisions that express her identity as a member of that group. She wants to emphasize Crossroads' uniqueness especially as compared to other Christian communities.

If her coworkers make fun of her, she does not really care. But if another church member hints that her contributions to the Crossroads ministries are not particularly important, she will find a way to respond. She may work harder to uphold the community's values and to demonstrate that she measures up to them. She may point out how poorly other churches or even certain other members of her own community live out their faith especially in the specific ways that Crossroads emphasizes. Sally expresses her group identity by pushing away people outside or on the fringes of the community and by stepping closer to the people in the center. A person with strong group ties, when made to feel like an outsider, responds by working harder to fit in.

	Sally, strongly connected	Joe, loosely connected
No threats	Expresses group identity	Concerned with accuracy and efficiency
Individually threatened	Heightens group behavior May attack others	Distances from group

NON-PERSECUTED GROUP BEHAVIOR[2]

The four different kinds of behaviors in not-very-persecuted churches just discussed can be expressed in either helpful or harmful ways. Like Joe, we all go through times when our commitment to our local church community is low, sometimes simply because we are new. Attendees who value efficiency push churches to raise their standards, which is ultimately a good thing. Individual differences are important, as well. It's okay to let outsiders know that our church affiliation is not the only thing that defines us. On the other hand, a concern for efficiency can become selfishness if our main focus is to get to church, worship God, and get out. Too much individualism can slide into stubbornness and rebellion—also evidences of selfishness.

Looking at Sally, we see some good things about identifying strongly with a congregation. Communities couldn't function if some people were not willing to work hard. Often, though, we think of people like Sally as the *best* Christians. When we devalue other churches also called by God, however, we can hurt the body of Christ as a whole. When our loyalty is challenged, recommitting ourselves to Christian service can strengthen our walk with God, but it should not happen at others' expense.

Each of these four scenes describes a reaction common in our communities. These behaviors aren't connected to a person's commitment to Christ. Instead they are related to the strength of the person's connection to the community and the presence or absence of outside pressures. How can knowing about these behaviors help us as we try to build strong communities but also maintain connections with those outside the church?

Questions:

1. Have you ever felt or behaved like Sally?

2. How do you react when your dedication to your community is questioned by another church member?

2. Ellemers, et al., "Self," 167.

3. Have you ever felt or behaved like Joe?

4. How do you react when someone from outside questions your church membership?

5. How could some of these reactions be helpful? How could they hurt?

PAUL AT THE INTERSECTION OF CHURCH AND CULTURE

Some of the communities that Paul founded did suffer persecution. In Philippi, after the conversion of Lydia and the exorcism of a slave girl, Paul and Silas were beaten and imprisoned, God sent an earthquake that brought the jailor to faith, and the magistrates discovered that Paul and Silas were Roman citizens and asked them to leave (Acts 16). Persecution continued after they left: "For it has been granted to you on behalf of Christ not only to believe on him, but also to suffer for him, since you are going through the same struggle you saw I had, and now hear that I still have" (Phil 1:29–30). During Paul's first visit to Ephesus, as well, the silversmiths reacted violently against his preaching, and although we are not sure of the full story, he mentions fighting wild beasts there and continued opposition (Acts 19; 1 Cor 15:32; 16:8–9).

In Corinth, though, Luke tells us that the local authorities refused to get involved even during a conflict with the synagogue (Acts 18). In Paul's letter to them, we see more evidence that the Corinthian followers of Christ, like us, were not-very-persecuted.

Paul makes many references in 1 Corinthians to situations that could only happen if followers of Christ interacted regularly and freely with other Corinthians. We read that outsiders could attend the community's gatherings, and followers of Christ were being invited into the homes of unbelievers (1 Cor 14:22–25; 10:27). Paul gave instructions to husbands and wives married to a person without faith in Christ, which could not have happened under persecution (1 Cor 7:13–15). The Corinthians that Paul wrote to went to court, and some of the men visited prostitutes (1 Cor 6:6; 6:15–20). The discussion about women's head coverings and the use of athletic imagery also show their connections with people of Corinth outside of their community (1 Cor 11:1–16; 9:24–27).

Sally wore Crossroads tee shirts to express her church identity. People in the Roman Empire might boast about their gifts or about how strong they were in Christ. Joe told his friends about the ways he was different from the people at Crossroads. Followers of Christ in Corinth might have gone to court or visited prostitutes to show other Corinthians that they were still good Romans.

Finally, Paul's letter shows that some followers of Christ expected to find the same values in the community that they were used to in the rest of their world. North Americans value efficiency, but Romans would have looked for opportunities for honor in a group with which they were loosely affiliated. Paul had to keep fighting that tendency to bring the values of the surrounding culture into the community. It is not just a matter of discerning sin. Followers of Christ have to re-evaluate everything.

Anyone who has lived in more than one culture knows what this kind of re-evaluation is like. Even international travel forces you to watch people who interact differently and figure out how to communicate with them. My family moved to Belgium when I was eight years old, so American culture often seems foreign to me. When I moved back in 1979, I remember asking my boyfriend to give me pop quizzes on the names of the Beatles. I didn't want to be caught without that essential knowledge that everyone but me seemed to have!

Table manners are different on opposite sides of the Atlantic, too. Mothers and fathers across the United States teach their children to fold their hands in their laps, while all over Belgium parents remind their kids to rest their wrists on the edge of the table. In adapting to American culture, I had to decide which Belgian manners to keep and which American ideals to accept. I learned pop culture references like the names of the four Beatles, I watched *Gone with the Wind,* and I didn't greet my American friends with a kiss on the right cheek, even though that had been perfectly appropriate in Belgium. But I continue to put my left wrist on the table and to hold my fork upside down.

The behaviors I was evaluating are neither holy nor sinful. Each is just a cultural expression of group identity on one continent or another. I knew that I needed to change enough to avoid offending people unintentionally, especially since I have an American accent and people expect me to know the unspoken codes. The way I eat, the way I cross my sevens, and probably other behaviors that I'm not entirely aware of, however, still make me a little different.

Although I thought carefully about my new identity when I came to live in the United States, we all do this same kind of identity construction almost unconsciously when we join a new group. We look at the way people dress, the way they speak, how close they stand to each other, and what topics of conversation they prefer. We then decide how much of this group identity we want to adopt, and how much of our previous identity we want to maintain.

Identity evaluation needs to happen as we move from our national culture into and out of our churches, too. Some values and behaviors should stay in place. We have to have enough in common with those outside the church to be able to interact with them. Other behaviors, although not sinful in themselves, have to be abandoned because they get in the way of God's call. As we build Christian communities, we have to re-evaluate the culture that we live in and possibly make changes according to the identity that the Bible tells us we should have.

We will look at group identity in more detail in the next chapter, but it's important to recognize here the balance that goes into this process of evaluation. The identity of our culture includes things like our independent spirit, our social divisions, and even our shopping habits. They will not necessarily change, nor will they change in the same way for every Christian. We will see, though, that Paul asks us to reshape them according to our calling and mission in Christ.

Paul stands at this intersection between church and culture, and in chapter 5 we will begin to look at what he has to say. First, we have to learn more from social science about common group behaviors, and take a look at Paul's background and the people who made up the community of Christ in Corinth.

Questions:

1. Read Acts 18:1—19:1. What does this background tell you about the followers of Christ in Corinth?

2. Review some of the areas where the Corinthian followers of Christ were interacting with other Corinthians.

3. When you interact with non-Christians, how well do you fit in with them?

4. What are some assumptions and behaviors that you share with the rest of your culture?

2

Who Are We?

Irv Holtzhouse III became Irv Van Wingerden when his mother was divorced and remarried, and his stepfather adopted him. He lost touch with his father's side of the family but never really connected with his new relatives. As a result, he carried a name that didn't fit.

Forty-four years later came a moment of decision: "I started to write my name down and I realized I didn't want to write Van Wingerden anymore." Now he is Irv Holtzhouse III once again.

What does his name mean to Irv? The Van Wingerdens valued level-headed business sense. Irv's desire to become a pastor, for example, "never made it with the Van Wingerdens but always would have been approved and encouraged by the Holtzhouses."

"When I took my name back, I really didn't even anticipate what it would be like," Irv says. "There was just such a sense of being home." At a recent Holtzhouse family reunion, he saw once again the tones, gestures, and expressions that he remembered from childhood. "For the first time in many, many years, I was welcomed with open arms. People were just very grateful and happy to see me." And now? Irv says, "I'm settled. It's good for me to be who I am."

~from an interview with Irv Holtzhouse III

WHEN WE TALK ABOUT identity, we usually mean the identity of an individual. *Who am I?* But that identity is affected, as Irv knows, by the people who surround us. *Who are we?* Our group memberships define us more than we may realize. When I learned about the various social processes that we will look at in this chapter, I could understand denominations better, see group dynamics at work in my church community, and evaluate my own motives more clearly. In addition, I began to see that these group identities often shape and are shaped by the words that we speak or write about ourselves and each other.

Group processes shaped the first century followers of Christ in Corinth, as well. Paul, of course, would not have used complex social scientific vocabulary in writing to them: "Corinthian followers of Christ, stop self-categorizing yourselves according to Roman identity! Your intragroup relationships are suffering, and your in-Christ identity lacks salience!"[1] Paul's words to the Corinthians would have had an impact on them, however. So if we look at some of the ways group identity works, we can then apply those insights to the first four chapters of 1 Corinthians.

INGROUPS AND OUTGROUPS

What do we mean when we talk about groups? At one time or another I have been a stay-at-home mom, a craft maker, a Boy Scout parent, an Awana parent, a Presbyterian, a Free Methodist, and a seminary student. Each name represents a group of other people I was connected to. They competed with other groups for my loyalty. After all, I could have chosen to be a working mom, a Christian Scientist, a basketball parent, a Baptist, or a golfer. Studies show that we look for groups of people who would accept us as members, and then we evaluate them based on our understanding of ourselves. We join those that fit us best.

Of course we belong to some groups without any decision on our part. I was born a woman and an American, and unless I take some significant steps, I will stay a part of those groups. Each of us belongs to a gender and a national culture which tends to remain stable over our lifetime whether we feel at home there or not. The expectations of these groups influence us, although we may also resist that influence. Those I connect with the most deeply will have the most impact on my identity.

Groups work to create community. Setting group standards, choosing characteristics the group values, establishing approved behaviors, all draw people together in a common bond. Each group will have specific expectations. At work, for example, personal space tends to be large and well respected. At a family reunion, though, if you keep those same

---

1. Although this chapter does explain these theories, we will try to avoid this language, as well!

boundaries, people may think you are distant, unfriendly, or even angry. Groups value vocabulary, clothing styles, jobs, and entertainment choices differently. If you identify strongly with the group, you will adopt many if not all of the expected behaviors. In any case, if you are a part of the group, you will feel the pressure to conform.

Why do we feel this pressure? Groups communicate their standards in a variety of ways. They may have a mission statement, bylaws, a pledge, or a membership covenant. These help members to understand the group's identity. They also allow visitors to evaluate the group and decide whether they will fit in.

More importantly, however, groups communicate their expectations through what they say about themselves and especially what they say about others. Called *outgroups,* these others show us who we are by defining for us who we are not. *They* have a great football team but *we* are committed to academics. *They* build wells in Africa but *we* feed the homeless. Democrats and Republicans, Anglicans and Baptists, men and women, talking about the *others* is often a way to define ourselves.

One way to talk about an outgroup is to describe the characteristics of that group. We take those characteristics and use them to create an imaginary person. If we carry the idea of that typical person in our head, we know how to treat someone from that group without being offensive. We won't ask a Muslim how she celebrated Easter. We know better than to tell a Baptist friend about the infant baptism last weekend, and we don't offer alcohol to a member of Alcoholics Anonymous. The picture of a typical person from another group helps us to understand people different from us and treat them well.

The typical people that we have imagined to help us relate to outsiders can turn into stereotypes, though. We may think that we already know all about someone from that group and have answers for their point of view. If we see each person as a carbon copy of the stereotype, we forget that they are unique individuals. We meet them and think, "Oh. You are one of *them*. I already know all about *you*." This stereotyping allows us to dismiss them. Instead of using this picture of others to give us information about them and to help us define ourselves in contrast to them, this process can build antagonism. *We* follow the Bible but *they* misinterpret. *We* work for social justice but *they* don't care about the poor. Outgroups become enemies and we become isolated.

A southern white friend once had to explain to a northerner that not all white southerners belonged to the Ku Klux Klan. Someone who looks Hispanic may have his citizenship questioned. Even a positive stereotype can be used to devalue someone else. If I believe, for example, that Asians are good at math, and I am not an Asian, then I have an excuse for my failure since math is not part of my genetic makeup. It's not my fault. On the other hand, I may judge the failure of someone who is Asian more harshly. She should have succeeded. Although developing the portrait of a typical member of a certain outgroup may help us to understand people different from us, we need to balance that with a reminder that each person of that outgroup is still an individual.

Outgroups help us to define ourselves because they contrast with us. When we tell each other the ways that we are different, we reinforce our own way of life. Outgroups, though, are usually surprisingly similar to us. It's easy to define our church in contrast to a Buddhist Temple; we are more likely to choose the church down the street as our primary outgroup. Pointing out differences does help us to communicate our group identity, but especially when we have so much in common, we have to be careful not to turn our outgroup into our enemy.

Questions:

1. List the various groups to which you belong. What does each group value?

2. Are there any groups where you might not be comfortable admitting your membership in another group?

3. What other groups do you compare yourselves to?

4. How is your group different from those other groups? How is it similar?

MODELS AND ROLES

In the same way that we create pictures of a typical member of outgroups, we also construct models of an ideal group member. A model may be a real person (a founder of the community, for example) or an imaginary person who has all the characteristics the group believes in. When a Boy Scout repeats, "A Scout is trustworthy, loyal, helpful, friendly, courteous, kind, obedient, cheerful, thrifty, brave, clean, and reverent," he builds a picture of a model Scout in his mind.[2] He will then measure his own behavior against that model.

Americans sometimes use Abraham Lincoln as a model of someone who started from humble beginnings and with honesty and perseverance, rose all the way to the presidency. He is the image of an independent, self-made man who stands for justice against oppression. He still represents the ultimate American for many people. When I got a big, soft toy horse for my second Christmas, I had already heard of him and named it "Abe Lincoln."

Other groups also have their role models. Political activists may look to Gandhi or Rosa Parks. Amy Carmichael and Hudson Taylor inspire missionaries; Michael Jordan and Serena Williams, athletes. Authors look to Jane Austen and Mark Twain; scientists, to George Washington Carver, Albert Einstein, and Marie Curie. The current leader or the original founder may become a group's model. We tell stories about these people. We carry them in our minds and measure ourselves against them. They remind us of the group standards and ideals.

In the same way that we saw with the stereotype of an outgroup, the process of creating models can lead to extremes. Instead of building unity, a group model can become not just a leader to copy but a cult ruler to worship and obey. Models can define a group so narrowly that they don't let anyone in. When new people try to join, they don't know the model well, and a tightly-knit church group may question these people's faith and treat them as if they carried some sort of disease.

When the process works well, a model person made up of the group ideals helps a community to shape its own identity. Talking about this person reinforces who they are. And although everyone in the group shares a commitment to this identity, each person takes on a specific role in the community.

Since we belong to many groups, we play many roles. I start a typical Thursday morning, for example, at the gym with my husband. If I'm awake enough on the drive, I may ask him about his day or share stories about mine. We discuss the family's schedule or a concern about one of the kids. During this time, I am mainly a wife.

2. Boy Scouts, *Handbook*, 33–34.

When I get home I am God's daughter during my devotional time and a home school mom when I teach my kids. I also plan lessons for my co-op class. In the afternoon when that class ends, I head for the seminary. There I will answer students' Greek questions and grade papers in my role as a teaching assistant. If I have a few free minutes, I may check out a book from the library for my research as a writer. At home again in the evening, I go back and forth as wife and mother unless I can also squeeze in some more writing time.

The specific ways I fulfill each role are shaped in part by the behavior of others. My idea of how a mother acts, for example, comes partly from my own mother, as well as other mothers I've seen and read about. I adapt those ideas, though, as my husband and I negotiate the way his idea of fatherhood overlaps, compliments, or conflicts with my idea of motherhood. As a co-op teacher, too, I have to figure out the expectations of the administration and the assumptions of the other teachers, the students, and their parents to decide what kind of a teacher I should be.

Who is the real Laura? Is she the writer? the wife? the mother? the teacher? All of these roles are a part of my identity. If I call my own mother in the evening or meet someone for coffee, then I am also a daughter or a friend. Each situation calls for another hat, another role. All of these roles line up like rungs on a ladder, switching in and out of the top position.

Questions:

1. Who are the role models for your groups?

2. How do they inspire you in good ways? How do they pressure you in bad ways?

3. What roles do you play?

4. How and when do they conflict with each other?

LADDERS AND WORDS

At any given moment, then, only the role at the top of the ladder is switched on. The others are still a part of my identity, but only the top one tells me what to do. When I go to school, I shift into teacher mode and when I come home I become a mom again. Some roles impact more people; others affect the people I care about the most. Studies have shown that these are the roles that have the greatest impact on my behavior. I spend a lot more time figuring out what kind of a mother I should be than I do deciding the best way to be the family's mail sorter. As I look back over my day, I see the switched-on identity changing so that I can behave correctly in each situation. I don't treat my husband like my student, nor my student like my son. Occasionally, however, my roles do collide. If one of my children calls me while I'm teaching or I run into my boss while at the movies with a friend, I may feel stressed as I figure out the right behavior in the middle of those very different roles.

All of the roles that we play move up and down the ladder, shifting in and out of the switched-on position. We then describe ourselves to others based on this identity, which may or may not have a title associated with it. One of my friends has the title of secretary at work, but at church, she is the woman who checks in with people on the fringes of the church community and finds out how they are doing and makes them feel welcome. This role is vital to the health of our church even though it has no title. We have a role in each of the groups we belong to.

Since we all belong to a variety of groups, we carry within us the expectations of each one. They form a ladder of identities, and the rungs of this ladder shift up and down, too. At the gym where good health is valued, I care a lot about how much weight I have gained or lost. At the church potluck, however, I may value fellowship more and help myself to a second piece of pie so that I can try Jennifer's, as well as John's. Some of these shifting values may include moral values like truthfulness or compassion, but they may also consist of cultural elements like clothing or body language. Since each group communicates its own identity, we shift the expectations up and down the ladder as we move from work to church to home. In each place, we adapt ourselves to fit in that environment.

The identities for our group memberships not only shift but sometimes conflict, as well. I noticed this especially when I joined the world of social networking. I post statuses that include jokes, quotes in academic languages, Bible verses, everyday events, and things that I think are funny.[3] The status line that works for one group of people doesn't work at all for others.[4] Do I want my professional colleagues to see my family's Christmas morning pictures? Will my pastor disapprove if I quote a line

3. Laura J. Hunt passed a pet grooming place on the way home today. They were also advertising "Fur Wood" for sale.

4. Christe lux mundi, qui sequitur te habebit lumen vitae.

from a funny movie? When group standards collide, we have to figure out which one gets priority.

So the groups we belong to and the roles we adopt affect our understanding of ourselves. We can imagine our identity arranged in two ladders with shifting rungs. The group and role at the top at any given moment are switched on. They control our behavior. The question that we will see Paul asking the Corinthians, however, and that we will need to ask ourselves is: How does God want to incorporate these identities in Christ?

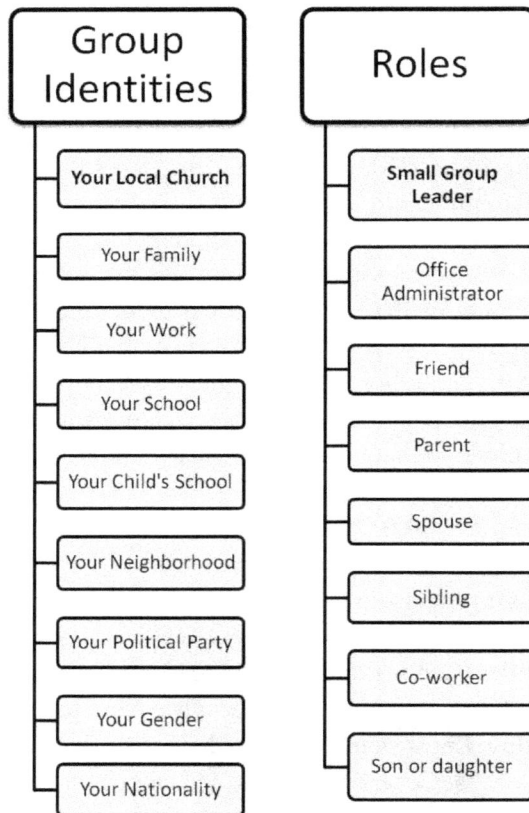

Group Identities	Roles
Your Local Church	Small Group Leader
Your Family	Office Administrator
Your Work	Friend
Your School	Parent
Your Child's School	Spouse
Your Neighborhood	Sibling
Your Political Party	Co-worker
Your Gender	Son or daughter
Your Nationality	

Group Identity and Role Ladders

Most of the time, we do this rung shifting without even thinking about it. It lets us move in and out of Christian and non-Christian groups, at least when persecution doesn't get in the way. We can bring the gospel to the world or invite the world into the church to experience the gospel. Sometimes, though, the rungs shift too well. Values that should stay switched on all the time, Christian values like honesty or service, move below getting ahead and getting along. We forget to live like Christians out there and start behaving like non-Christian Americans in here. Our models overlap or switch at the wrong time. Paul has to help the Corinthians stay in balance. They shouldn't abandon all contact with Roman Corinth, but they have to be more careful about bringing Roman Corinth into their community of followers of Christ.

Paul solves these problems by writing to the Corinthians. Words written down can be read over and over again. Certain words, certain topics, can help a group of people to reshape their identity. Starting in chapter 5, we will watch the way that works in 1 Corinthians 1—4. In the meantime, we can look at some of these processes at work throughout the Bible.

Words like steadfastness, courage, strength, and love shape the identity of the people of God (1 Cor 16:13–14). They contribute to our understanding of who we are.

The Bible uses outgroups to show us behaviors to avoid, as well. When the Bible lists "the acts of the sinful nature," it describes our outgroup (Gal 5:19–21). We use this information to define ourselves as *not them*. The Canaanites, the Egyptians, the Philistines, and gentile sinners all provide negative examples (Lev 18:24; Lev 18:3; Isa 2:6; Matt 6:7). We look at them and see what *not* to do.

Examples of people who broke the pattern of certain outgroups keep us from turning outgroups into enemies. Ruth was a Moabite and Nicodemus was a Pharisee (Ruth 1:4; John 3:1). Positive examples of individual outsiders remind us that we have to relate to others one person at a time.

The Bible gives us models to follow, too. Abraham left everything in response to God's call. Ruth stayed faithful. Jesus sacrificed himself for his enemies. Mary humbly obeyed. Paul preached the gospel in the face of persecution (Gen 12:4; Ruth 1:16; Rom 5:8; Luke 1:38; Acts 16). As we tell each other their stories, we reinforce the behavior appropriate for God's people and absorb them into our identity.

The models in the Bible are not perfect, though, except for Jesus. David and Peter made some serious mistakes along with many great choices (2 Sam 11; Matt 26). Some individuals among God's people provide completely negative examples, as well. Cain allowed jealousy to push him to murder (Gen 4:4–8). Judas betrayed the Son of God (Matt 27:3–5). Ananias and Sapphira lied (Acts 5:1–11). Simon the Magician believed and was baptized, but then he thought he could buy spiritual gifts (Acts 8:9–24). In each of these cases, a member of the community, someone who should have been a role model, shows flaws that help to keep us from idolizing any person other than Jesus or identifying too strongly with any one ingroup.

We will see in Corinth, too, people who struggled with ingroups, outgroups, models, and ladders. Because they were not persecuted, Corinthians could continue to do business with people without faith in Christ. This could help to communicate the gospel, but it also got in the way of the people's identity as followers of Christ. The community's definition of itself carried too much of the identity of the outside world. But before we can look at the ways Paul addresses these problems in 1 Corinthians, we have to find out more about Paul himself.

Questions:

1. Which of your roles switch and sometimes clash?

2. What behaviors do you change to adapt to the groups you belong to?

3. Which of those changes are helpful? Which of those changes might not be?

4. Where do you see the Bible creating the identity of God's people by giving characteristics, creating models, or pointing to outgroups?

3

Who Was Paul?

I was raised in a fairly typical Jewish family just outside of London, England. Apart from a few traditions, my family was not truly focused on Judaism or the Bible. Once every year, though, our extended family would gather for the Passover. We would recount the Exodus story and partake in the symbolic elements of the feast.

I remember the aifikomen *most vividly. Three pieces of unleavened bread are wrapped and separated by cloth. At a specific point in the ceremony, the head of the house removes the middle piece, a traditional prayer is recited, and it is broken in two. One half is returned and the other is given a special name, the* aifikomen, *which means,* that which comes later, *and that is exactly what happens. The* aifikomen *is wrapped in a white cloth and hidden somewhere in the house. Later the children search for it; it must be found before the ceremony can conclude. I knew that if I found it, I would get a prize. So it was definitely worth finding!*

Some years later through reading the New Testament for the first time I came to know Jesus as the Jewish Messiah and my personal savior. In the Jewish-Christian congregation, Passover was celebrated in light of the fulfillment that came through the true Passover lamb, the Messiah Jesus. At the point in the service when the middle piece of unleavened bread was broken, it was explained that the three pieces represent the three persons of the trinity: the Father, the Son, and the Holy Spirit. When I saw the middle piece removed, broken, and then buried, it became clear to me that this was a symbol of our Messiah who came from heaven, was broken for our sins, and buried. Then, when the aifikomen *was found, I realized that this portrayed Jesus, raised from the grave, resurrected, overcoming the power of death for eternity.*

This strange custom that I celebrated as a child but never knew the true meaning of now became so clear. It was a symbol, a representation of our Messiah Jesus, broken, buried, and then raised from the dead, so that all of us may live.

~ condensed with permission from a private email from Elliot Marks

PAUL'S BACKGROUND

Each of us connects with a different person in the Bible. Some of us really enjoy Peter. His impulsive nature and his tendency to speak without thinking feel familiar. We are encouraged when we see Jesus forgive him and send him out again after his failures.

But Paul is a little different. He thinks before he speaks . . . and thinks and thinks and thinks. He analyzes a problem until he sees it as a thorn in the flesh sent to prevent pride (2 Cor 12:7). He agonizes over his fellow Jews' blindness to Christ until he wishes that he, himself, could be cursed if it would help them (Rom 9:3). He usually argues logically although he has a tendency towards sarcasm (Romans; 1 Cor 4:8). And in an era when letters were usually shorter than Jude, he wrote Romans and 1 Corinthians, pages and pages containing "some things that are hard to understand" (2 Pet 3:16). Ultimately, however, he says, "by the grace of God, I am what I am" (1 Cor 15:10).

To understand Paul better, we need to look at the groups he belonged to. He tells us that he was a descendent of Benjamin, a "Hebrew of Hebrews" (Phil 3:5). He was a man, of course, living in the Roman Empire, an inhabitant of Tarsus in Cilicia (Acts 22:27; 21:39), and part of the class of manual laborers (Acts 18:3).

In those various groups, he had roles to play. He was a student, a Roman citizen, and a tentmaker. On the day that he met Jesus on the road to Damascus, the role on the top rung of his ladder would have been *zealous destroyer of heretics* (Gal 1:13–14), and his topmost group identity would have been *Pharisee, eager for God* (Acts 22:3).

Some scholars now argue that Paul did not think of that experience on the Damascus road as a conversion.[1] What happened there was instead a fulfillment and reorientation of Paul's worldview. He did not convert away *from* Judaism. Instead, he met Jesus in whom God was reconciling the whole world to himself as the prophets had foretold (2 Cor

1. For more about this debate see Zetterholm, *Approaches*.

5:19; Ps 22:27). Paul's role changed from destroyer of heretics to God's slave in his mission to bring news of this reconciliation to the gentiles (2 Cor 5:18–20).

Meeting Jesus changed Paul's group identity somewhat but did not completely replace it. When Paul prayed at the temple and fulfilled vows, he was living as a Jew (Acts 18:18; 21:20–26; 22:17). In addition, Paul used Old Testament quotations in the kind of analytical style that he would have learned "at the feet of Gamaliel," so his identity as a Pharisee continued to a certain degree, as well (Acts 22:3). However, he changed his understanding of food laws and of whether and how Jews and gentiles could eat together (Gal 2:11–14). He had to make room for including gentiles, as gentiles, among the people of God. Jeremiah, a prophet to the gentiles, seems to have become one of Paul's new role models (Jer 1:5; Gal 1:15–16; 2:8). The Jewish role of Rabbi and the Greek tradition of a traveling orator also provided models for him as he answered God's call to become an apostle to the gentiles. Maybe by the time he went to Corinth, his identity looked something like this:

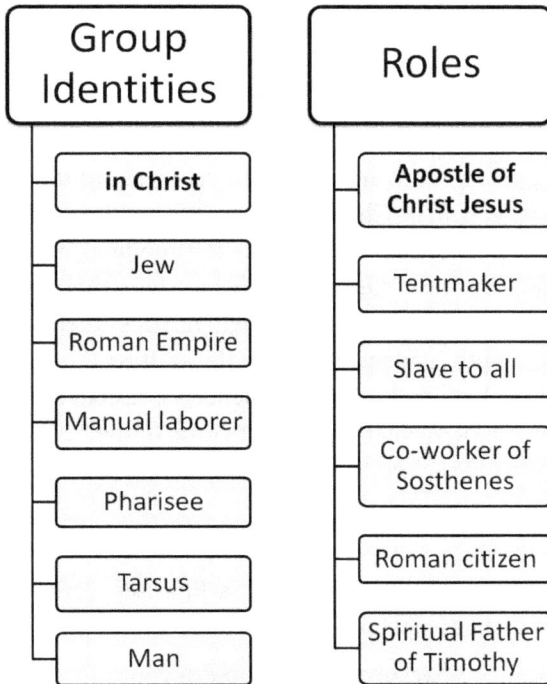

Group Identities	Roles
in Christ	Apostle of Christ Jesus
Jew	Tentmaker
Roman Empire	Slave to all
Manual laborer	Co-worker of Sosthenes
Pharisee	Roman citizen
Tarsus	Spiritual Father of Timothy
Man	

Paul's Group Identity and Role Ladders

Paul's view of the world was centered on the worship of the one holy creator God of Israel, and it did not change very much although he did have to adapt to his new revelation of Jesus as God. But we can see his shift in identity as similar to that of someone who was raised in a Christian family—not the same kinds of changes but similar in number. If you grew up going to church, you knew the Bible and you had some understanding of God, Jesus, and the Holy Spirit. Still, you probably found as an adult that some of the foundations that you had laid, some of your values, your identity, or your role models had to change as you made your parents' faith your own.

Some Christians say that they thought as children that Christianity meant following rules. As adults they realized that following rules should come from knowing Jesus, which is the more important value. So their identity shifted from one based on rules to one based on a relationship.

Sometimes these identity shifts happen little by little as Christian children grow up. My young daughter once told me that as a preschooler she had watched the other kids and figured out that being a Christian girl meant being good and being the most popular. She spoke to me very seriously later on as she explained her discovery that Christianity actually had nothing to do with popularity.

Looking at the way a child's Christian faith develops into adulthood, paying attention to the shifts in values, outgroups, models, and roles that happen as a person's faith matures, and recognizing the importance of these moments can help Christians who don't think they have a testimony. Because we normally describe a testimony as a before and after story, lifelong Christians often feel unable to share their faith. Telling the story of these times of growth, though, will impact others who are finding their childhood faith inadequate to handle adult realities.

Some of us, like Paul, have experienced a reshaping of our identity that left in place a lot of what was there before. In the next section, we will look at the words Paul used to talk about this new identity.

Questions:

1. How would Paul's background as a Pharisaic Jew help him in his new role as an apostle of Christ?

2. How does your background help you in your life as a Christian?

3. What kinds of things had to change for Paul when he met Jesus?

4. What has changed for you as you have developed your relationship with Christ as an adult?

PAUL IN CHRIST

When Paul writes to the Corinthians, he uses one phrase over and over, thirteen times in the first letter: 'in Christ' (1 Cor 1:2, 4, 30; 3:1; 4:10, 15, 17; 15:18, 19, 22, 31; 16:24). The followers of Jesus are in Christ. They are sanctified in Christ, infants in Christ, and wise in Christ. They hope in Christ. Grace is given in Christ. Those who die have fallen asleep in Christ and will be made alive in Christ. They have guardians in Christ, but Paul is their father in Christ. His way of life is in Christ. He glories over the Corinthians in Christ, and he sends love to all of them in Christ.

The word 'Christian' was not commonly used in Paul's day. In the Bible, it is only mentioned in Acts 11:26; 26:28; and 1 Pet 4:16. Followers of Christ were sometimes called followers of the Way (Acts 24:14). But 'in Christ' seems to be the term for Christian identity that Paul likes best. This identity should reshape but not replace all the previous ones.

James Dunn, a British New Testament scholar, suggests that Paul uses this phrase in three slightly different ways.[2] First, 'in Christ' can refer to the specific things which Jesus Christ has accomplished. When Paul says that grace was given in Christ, he means that we have this grace as a result of Jesus' life and death (1 Cor 1:4–9). In Romans 3:24, Paul talks about redemption in Christ Jesus, that is, redemption that we have as a result of his work. This use points towards the past. Because we are in Christ, we are connected with what he has done.

Secondly, 'in Christ' refers to the standing that Christ's work gives to his followers in the present. Not only did Jesus accomplish his own mission, but he has now invited all of humanity to live in him. This new identity changes our values. When Paul told the Corinthians that they were in Christ, told them about their sanctification in Christ, and called them infants in Christ, he was describing the present reality of this new community, giving it shape, and moving this identity up their ladder (1 Cor 1:30; 1:2; 3:1).

---

2. Dunn, *Paul*, 396–401.

The last meaning of 'in Christ' relates to the future. Because of the grace given in Christ (first meaning), because of Paul's new 'in Christ' identity (second meaning), he now has a mission in Christ. In Christ, Paul has become a father to the Corinthians (1 Cor 4:15), and he expects the Corinthians to live in Christ, as well. They, too, should see themselves as a part of a mission in Christ to the world.

'In Christ,' then, identifies followers of Jesus. Although these past, present, and future meanings overlap, they help us to see the broad impact that an 'in Christ' identity should have. People who belong to this group will add this new mission to their ladder.

Paul was able to welcome the Corinthians to this mission because he knew the prophecies that promised that the nations would someday be included among the people of God (Ps 86:9; Zeph 2:11; Zech 14:16). He saw that Jesus' life, death, and resurrection enabled the fulfillment of these prophecies. As a result, gentiles could worship the God of Israel without becoming Jews. However, Paul could still point out areas where the gentiles needed to reshape their former identity for life in Christ.

If you, like the Corinthians and like me, came to Christianity from a completely different worldview, you may have gone through this identity shift. I remember that as a young teen I came up with logical, rational reasons to believe in God. (For one thing, if there's even a possibility that the Bible could be true, the existence of God is definitely the side to bet on!) Once I settled that question, though, I sighed, "Okay, it's nice to know that I believe in God, but what I really need is a friend."

When I met Jesus, I discovered that he was both God and friend. I would encourage anyone who has not yet met him to ask forgiveness for the sinfulness you carry and the sins you have committed, to thank him for Jesus' death on the cross that bridges the separation between us and God, and to ask for the Holy Spirit to come and show you how to live a life of worship to him. After that, it's important to find other Christians to grow with. This new community will reshape previous identities, adding and explaining who we are in Christ.

Questions:

1. How would a gentile's identity change in Christ?

2. How does someone's past, present, and future change in Christ?

3. How much did your values change in Christ?

4. What stayed the same?

PAUL'S PURPOSE IN 1 CORINTHIANS

Paul first came to Corinth sometime around A.D. 50, and Luke describes his visit in Acts 18. Paul stayed with Aquila and Priscilla, and they taught in the synagogues until they were forced out. After that he continued to teach there to a mostly gentile community for at least a year and a half (Acts 18:6).

Paul then went to Ephesus with Aquila and Priscilla. After some more traveling, he came back to Ephesus, and from there he kept in touch with the Corinthian community through letters and reports from other travelers (1 Cor 5:9; 7:1; 1 Cor 1:11; 5:1). By about A.D. 54, then, Paul writes 1 Corinthians to a community that he has founded, that he knows well, and with whom he has a continuing relationship.

When we look at the letter from the perspective of group identity, we see that the Corinthian followers of Christ had begun to lose the vision and values that should have defined them. The priorities of the surrounding culture had slipped in. This may also have affected the way community members understood and applied the instructions that Paul had given them. Their 'in Christ' identity was no longer on the top rung.

When Paul wrote to the Corinthians, then, he needed to let them know that, on the one hand, (and unlike what some may have been teaching) they could keep their gentile identity. Some of their behavior would still be based on old priorities. However, other old values would conflict with their new identity as followers of Christ. In those cases, their understanding of themselves would have to change.

When we look at 1 Corinthians as a whole, we can see some of the group processes that we talked about in the last chapter. Paul addresses issues of identity in several passages of the letter. In each case, he gives the Corinthians a piece of their identity in Christ that should fix the problems in their community if they will include it in their top rung.

> For since in the wisdom of God the world through its wisdom did not know him, God was pleased through the foolishness of what was preached to save those who believe. Jews demand miraculous signs and Greeks look for wisdom, but we preach Christ crucified: a stumbling block to Jews and foolishness to gentiles, but to *those whom God has called*, both Jews and Greeks, Christ the power of God and the wisdom of God. For the foolishness of God is wiser

than man's wisdom, and the weakness of God is stronger than man's strength. 1 Cor 1:21–25 (emphasis mine)

We will look more closely at this passage in chapter 6, but we see here signs of a division between Jewish and gentile followers of Christ. Were the gentiles valuing wisdom too highly? Were the Jews making miracles a test of orthodoxy? Maybe people from the surrounding culture were watching the followers of Christ and looking for wisdom and miracles. That might make them feel that they had to live up to those expectations. The divisions could not have been too serious or the early community would not have survived. Apparently, though, wisdom and miracles had become ways for those in the community to measure each other and to rank themselves. These were the values on the top rung of their ladder.

But Paul does not discount wisdom or miracles. After all, later in this same letter he says, "You are in Christ Jesus, who has become for us wisdom from God" (1 Cor 1:30) and, "My message and my preaching were . . . with a demonstration of the Spirit's power" (1 Cor 2:4). Paul values wisdom as God defines it, and he recognizes the place of miracles even in his own ministry. However, when he sees that these things have become more important to the Corinthians than the calling in Christ that they all have received, Paul asks them to re-evaluate their ladder of identity. Followers of Christ should have wisdom and they should accomplish miracles, but those abilities should not bring more honor in the community than the amazing reality that each one has been called by the voice of the Son of God.

> Nevertheless, each one should retain the place in life that the Lord assigned to him and to which God has called him. This is the rule I lay down in all the churches. Was a man already circumcised when he was called? He should not become uncircumcised. Was a man uncircumcised when he was called? He should not be circumcised. Circumcision is nothing and uncircumcision is nothing. *Keeping God's commands* is what counts. Each one should remain in the situation which he was in when God called him. Were you a slave when you were called? Don't let it trouble you—although if you can gain your freedom, do so. For he who was a slave when he was called by the Lord is the Lord's freedman; similarly, he who was a free man when he was called is Christ's slave. You were bought at a price; do not become slaves of men. Brothers, each man, as responsible to God, should remain in the situation God called him to. 1 Cor 7:17–24 (emphasis mine)

Here we see again Paul reminding the Corinthians of their priorities. In the social world of Corinth, the groups mentioned here (the circumcised and the uncircumcised, the slaves and the free) would each have an established status. Since bathing was a regular communal practice, circumcision or uncircumcision would be obvious. (Celsus, a Roman writing at about this time, describes a process for reversing circumcision "for the sake of appearance.") Slavery was not tied to race, but slaves would still be recognized by marks of abuse and sometimes by tattoos, chains, or shaved heads. Roman protocol would have dictated treating these people as inferior. Each group would have been the outgroup for another. If high-status Corinthian followers of Christ kept their Roman values at the top of their ladder of identity, they might have snubbed those *others* even during worship. Those *others* would continue to honor those of high status despite their common calling in Christ. Paul writes to point out that although these differences exist, giving and receiving honor should not rank more highly in their identity than their response to God's call: keeping God's commands.

> So whether you eat or drink or whatever you do, do it all for *the glory of God*. Do not cause anyone to stumble, whether Jews, Greeks or the church of God—even as I try to please everybody in every way. For I am not seeking my own good but the good of many, so that they may be saved. Follow my example, as I follow the example of Christ. 1 Cor 10:31–33 (emphasis mine)

Here again Paul recognizes the differences within the community but reminds the followers of Christ to see those differences in light of God's call to spread the good news. Jews and Greeks, both inside and outside of the community, would have had different customs which Paul urges them to respect. The Corinthians' old role models would have emphasized the differences of the outgroups and encouraged each group to work for its own good. Paul tells them that he replaces those models because he models himself on Christ. They teach that cultural preferences should rank lower in this new identity than the glory of God and the salvation of many.

> The body is a unit, though it is made up of many parts; and though all its parts are many, they form one body. So it is with Christ. For we were all baptized by one Spirit into one body—whether Jews or

Greeks, slave or free—and *we were all given the one Spirit* to drink.
1 Cor 12:12–13 (emphasis mine)

In this last example, Paul once again calls the Corinthians to give their differences a lower priority than the things which unify them. In context, Paul has just discussed the different gifts of God's Spirit. Now he includes cultural (Jew or Greek) and social (slave or free) identities among the differences. Like the various spiritual gifts, these differences can't (and shouldn't) go away. (To give a present-day example, a German immigrant who joins an American church will be culturally different, no matter how devoted to Christ.) But the common experience of the Spirit, Paul says, should allow the community to work as one body. Unity in Christ come first but does not destroy unique differences.

These passages also bring up the way Paul's Jewish identity might have caused some confusion among his converts about how gentile followers of Christ should behave. They probably assumed that they should imitate him in everything. So Paul wrote to somewhat adjust their understanding of this model. He tells them that they should not adopt Jewish customs, but neither could they continue to keep their previous values, such as honor, wisdom, and power. An identity in Christ is going to look a little different than their old identity. Paul also wrote to the Jewish followers of Christ to remind them that their Jewish identity did not give them more respect than the gentile converts. He wrote to slaves to reassure them that they did not have a low status in the community. He wrote to the rest to remind them that they, too, were now slaves. Honor in this new identity is handled differently than in the identity promoted by the Roman Empire.

In all four of these passages, Paul is discussing the social identity of the Corinthian followers of Christ. His own values and roles had shifted, and the words he wrote worked to reshape their group identity, as well. But who were these Corinthians that Paul was writing to? What did this early community look like? In the next chapter, we will examine the social status and the values of these followers of Christ.

Questions:

1. What gives people status in your Christian community? How does remembering that God has called each person put those differences in perspective?

2. What different places in life do people in your community have? How does remembering that the most important thing is obeying God's commandments put those differences in perspective?

3. What are some of the different habits of people in your community? How does remembering that they can work together to accomplish God's mission put those differences in perspective?

4. What different gifts do you see in your community? How does remembering that they were given by the same Holy Spirit put those differences in perspective?

5. How could Paul's reminders help us to accept our differences and create unity in our community?

4

Who Were the Corinthians?

*Greetings from the federal assembly of the Lycians and the Lycian
magistrates to the magistrates, the council, and the people of
Corinth. By an honorific decree made in favor of Junia Theodora,
living among you, it is voted to grant her both the crowning with a
golden crown and the offering of a portrait for her deification after
her death, and we have sent you a copy (of the decree) sealed with
the public seal so as to inform you at the same time. . . .*

*[The] portrait [is] painted on a gilt background and engraved
with the following inscription: "The federal assembly of the Lycians
and the Lycian magistrates have honored with a crown and a portrait painted on a gilt background Junia Theodora, a Roman, living
at Corinth, a fine and honorable woman and constantly devoted to
the nation by reason of her affection."*

*~An inscription from the first century,
one of five found at the gravesite of Junia Theodora*[1]

To understand 1 Corinthians, we not only have to know something about Paul, but we also need a glimpse of Paul's world. In this
chapter we will look at the history, the people, and the culture of Corinth
during the first century A.D., from the perspective of a freed slave, a
wealthy woman, and a retired Roman soldier. Through their eyes, we can
see the values of family, of honor and shame, and of wisdom in the Roman

---

1. Translation slightly adapted from Kearsley, "Women," 206–7.

Empire. We can then picture the people who made up the community of followers of Christ that Paul was writing to.

SOCIAL STATUS IN CORINTH

If you were living in Corinth in Paul's day, you would most likely have been a slave or one of the poor. Many slaves lived comfortably with, unlike the poor, the guarantee of a daily meal; however, they were seen as physical extensions of their owners without rights even over their own bodies. Some slaves had opportunities for advancement and education, but others suffered under terrible living conditions in mines or on farms.

The connection between owner and slave continued by law even after a slave was freed, which seems to have happened fairly frequently. Previous owners were responsible to give their former slaves financial advice, to make sure they never starved, and to pursue justice if they were murdered. In return, slaves continued to honor their previous masters and to provide various services for them. They were forbidden to sue them and had to give them a share of any legacy they might leave behind.

If your master did free you or if you earned the money to buy your way out of slavery, you would be one among the many freedmen in the Corinthian population, which stood at about 80,000. When the Roman colony of Corinth was founded, it was populated with freed slaves, and they and their descendants struggled for honor in a culture which valued a family name. Although you might have proven yourself capable by your successful business practices, and you might have as much money as a retired Roman soldier, you would not have the same status.

One solution would be to run for public office. To get votes, you must provide benefits for the citizens of the city. Various inscriptions show the public buildings and monuments that were paid for in this way. One freedman had carved (not once, but twice!) on a small structure in the marketplace of Corinth: "Gnaeus Babbius Philinus, aedile and pontifex, had this monument erected at his own expense, and he approved it in his official capacity of duovir."[2] When I read this, I always think, "My name is G. B. Philinus, and I approve this message."

Holding an office would not only bring you honor, it would also allow you to give favors to those closest to you. You could supply jobs or

---

2. Aedile, pontifex, and duovir were titles like city planning director, priest, and city attorney. Murphy-O'Connor, *Corinth*, 270.

access to the courts for your family and friends, and you could do favors for less honorable members of society. This would set up a give-and-take relationship with them. You, as a patron, would give them money or invite them to dinners. They, as your clients, would benefit from association with you, sharing in your glory, but also increasing your honor by their numbers, their votes, and their loyalty.

The patron-client relationship extended all the way through the various levels of society. As a freed slave, your former master acts as a patron to you, but you could have clients, as well. Even a wealthy Roman citizen would see the emperor as his patron, bestowing favors on the colony of Corinth in exchange for the honor paid to him.

A wealthy woman would have similar struggles with status. She might have money but advancement would be difficult. The patron-client relationship would provide a way for her to gain honor. The opening quotation for this chapter tells us about Junia Theodora who lived in Corinth in the first century. The Lycians praise her generosity, her hospitality, and the way she helped them by "assuring the friendship of the authorities which she seeks to win by every means." Inscriptions of this kind show that a few Roman women did have money, influence, and independence. As a patron, she would expect to be honored, whether in writing (as here) or simply by the way her clients would promote her wherever they went.

The hospitality of a patron would also include meals. These could be formal affairs where those of higher status got the best seats and often the best food. As a patron, this would give you the opportunity to display your wealth. Even slaves and the slaves of the guests would be given places at the lower tables. The more people you could feed the higher your status.

At the top of the social scale, we would find the retired Roman soldier and his descendants. If you were one of them, you would remember that 200 years ago, your ancestors wiped out the inhabitants of this area and destroyed the city. One hundred years ago, it was refounded by your most illustrious ancestor, Julius Caesar, descended from the goddess Venus. You are proud that the city has recently regained the title of provincial capital. You stand at an important crossroad; ships use this narrow piece of land (see B3, marked Isthmus with an arrow on the map), to move their goods from the Italian side of the Mediterranean to the Egyptian side, saving time and avoiding the stormy open waters. Your city provides everything visiting sailors and merchants, as well as land travelers going north and south might need.

Map Base © 2011, Ancient World Mapping Center (www.unc.edu/awmc)

Some descendents of the conquered Greeks still live here, but the important members of society, of which you are a part, are Roman citizens and speak Latin. Your people have an impressive genealogy which you trace back through the tribes of early Rome to connect with the Trojans and the ancient Greek story of the Trojan War. You admire the remains of the Greek structures here in Corinth, and whenever possible you support restoring them with, of course, improvements.

You enjoy the luxuries that your wealth and position entitle you to. You provide lavish dinners that include oysters and turtledoves with mushrooms, and you invite your friends, your clients, and the poor. You live according to the saying of the Stoics, "That you may be wise, strive toward a sound mind at top speed and with your whole strength." You try to cultivate this kind of calmness of mind.

You own slaves, and several of them have served you well and developed skills which would allow them to live independently. One, in particular, has become a fairly successful fishmonger, and you are considering allowing him to buy his freedom.[3] His elevation would reflect well on you. On the other hand, you are concerned that the new wet nurse you bought

3. Theissen, *Pauline Christianity*, 157.

for your grandson might not be of high enough quality. (A later Roman, Favorinus, would say on this subject, "Shall we then allow this child of ours to be infected with some dangerous contagion and to draw a spirit into its mind and body, from a body and mind of the worst character?"[4]) But in general you are pleased with the way your household is running.

This intentionally multi-layered society sounds different to Americans who, at least in theory, believe that "all men are created equal." Some parts of this description may sound familiar, though. Our nation, too, was built after the destruction of an earlier civilization. Some of us trace our ancestry back to the conquerors, and yet we tell the stories of Pocahontas, Sacagawea, and Sitting Bull the way the Romans remembered and admired the Greeks. Others of us, like the Greeks in Corinth, descend from the conquered, and have lived with loss of status in a civilization we did not create. Corinth, like the United States, had immigrants who fled persecution or economic hardship and arrived like Priscilla and Aquila, hoping to establish a business, bringing their religion with them.

Americans, like Romans, have a tendency to see themselves as the civilized ones, as opposed to other cultures which we may believe have some quirks and oddities that need straightening out. In more recent times, we have tried to broaden our perspective but we are still known internationally for comments that show a lack of respect. When my brother lived in England, he visited Dover Castle with its stone stairs worn by 800 years of footsteps. Two elderly American women grumbled about their unevenness: "They would never allow this back home!" Romans, too, thought of themselves as the judges of what should be allowed and what should not.

Less familiar would be the Roman emphasis on family name. Some of us research our genealogies, but we generally take more credit for what we accomplish ourselves than for what our fathers did. Like the Romans, however, we may seek honor with large donations and found a library or a college building that carries our name. Job perks in America don't usually include benefits for family and friends. But other cultures in our world today may expect that an adult who works for the government, for example, will use that position to benefit his relatives, so that kind of system is not unknown. We generally don't give gifts and expect a return on the investment later, but that kind of exchange does happen. So although the

---

4. Glancy, *Slavery*, 18–19. Much of the information on slavery in this chapter also comes from Glancy.

society of ancient Corinth is foreign to us, we can find a few connections to help us imagine it more clearly.

These examples of the various levels of Corinthian society show us the world in which Paul was writing. People struggled with status and found ways to advance. A group that consisted of members of all of these different classes would be hard to unite. The language of the Roman Empire offered Paul some expressions that he could use to call the followers of Christ together.

Questions:

1. Which of the people of Corinth do you most identify with?

2. Describe that person to the rest of the group.

3. How have you seen status, name, rank, or position respected, or the lack of it disrespected?

4. What other things do we respect or disrespect in our culture?

VALUES IN CORINTH

We all use language to promote group identity. When we call someone a brother or a sister, when we praise or ridicule someone, when we talk about the way to make good decisions (which the Romans would call wisdom), we communicate the values that we find important. In the Roman Empire, the language of family made the rule of the emperors legitimate. The language of honor and shame both supported the status of the elite and provided honor for those who otherwise had less. The language of wisdom strengthened the Romans' connection with the glories of their past and gave them a moral foundation for present life. By understanding some of this vocabulary, we will better understand Paul's words to the followers of Christ in Corinth.

About 75 years before Paul, Emperor Augustus had presented himself as the father of the fatherland and therefore as a role model for moral behavior. This let him carry out reforms across all of the various peoples in his empire, bringing them together into one family. Lines were traced through fathers, but ironically, the emperors themselves were only related through the sisters and wives of previous rulers. Adoption became a way to create legal succession. Three out of the four emperors in the early first century adopted the man who became the next emperor either as their son or grandson.

Emperors extended their control by adding religious language to that of family. Augustus made his father, Julius Caesar, a god, so the worship of each successive emperor became a logical next step. At first they were believed to become gods when they died, but later emperors accepted worship during their lifetimes. What we would think of as patriotism today was religion then. Corinth was named the "colony of Corinth in praise of Julius," pointing to the cult of the emperor there. An inscription from the middle of the first century mentions Spartiaticus, a "priest of the divine Julius." Statues, temples, and coins with the emperor's picture would remind the people of his presence during everyday life.

Roman emperors, then, connected family with religion and extended their families beyond parents and children. These practices were reflected at every level of society. Household gods had some association with family ancestors, and the line between a household (with slaves and servants) and a family was often blurred. Patrons would act as fathers to their clients. Voluntary associations, based on a common trade or the worship of a particular god or goddess, might also use the language of brotherhood. The Romans had conquered many different peoples who may not have been truly united, but the language of family would call them together. It communicated a common group identity and created a sense of belonging. We will see that Paul uses similar words to unite the Corinthian followers of Christ.

The language of honor and shame worked within the system of patronage to build unity, as well. Gift giving could enhance a wealthy person's honor. Shame, too, is a powerful motivator. Even if a person cannot reach the status of one specially honored, he or she will take care not to act in ways that bring shame.

Think about the times you have done or not done something because you cared what others thought of you—maybe you didn't mention a television show you watch because people would make fun of you, or you talked about your travels because you thought people would admire you. This pull towards doing the things which would gain honor and avoiding the things which would bring shame was one of the main mechanisms operating in first century society. As we saw in the second chapter, this kind of pressure is not necessarily bad. Honor and shame simply call group members to conform to group standards.

The concept of grace was a vital part of the patronage system and therefore important to the outworking of honor and shame. Grace described three things: the patron's gift, the gift itself, and the gratitude of the client. Seneca, a Stoic philosopher and contemporary of Paul, described these three aspects of grace with the analogy of three women holding hands and dancing in a circle.[5] The constant movement in harmony created the beauty of the system.

This meant that each person had a role to play, a specific orientation of the heart which would allow the dance to continue. The patron was to give benefits liberally and openheartedly. He might search out those most likely to be thankful, but he must not give reluctantly. If he met with ingratitude, he must not for that reason stop giving. The client, on the other hand, should respond with gratitude, and that gratitude itself would grow with more openhearted giving. This was the ideal direction for the dance.

In practice, however, patrons might give to receive the praise that would enhance their public honor. Clients might accept gifts to attach themselves to important men, thus increasing their own importance. They might also offer public praise to their patrons in the hopes of receiving more benefits. Although ideally all hearts would be turned in one direction, in practice the dance might proceed in the opposite direction entirely. Still, generosity and gratitude were the ideals.

Roman culture also valued wisdom. Pupils memorized the philosophy of the teacher and learned the skills of public speaking. Teachers might travel to various assemblies, to the forums, or to athletic contests, where they would offer their wisdom to those who would listen.

This wisdom presented rules for ordering one's life and society. Following wisdom would allow rulers to rule well, members of society to find their proper place, and all to accept the events of life as fate. Occasionally rivalries would develop between different speakers and their followers as they competed for public attention.

While these teachers were valued in part because of their speaking abilities, some sold their skills to the highest bidder. They were ironically called the wise ones, *sophists*. They might hire themselves out to argue any point of view. Although they had ability, their lack of integrity made them suspect, and poetry and plays regularly made fun of them.

5. DeSilva, *Themes*, 8.

Wisdom established the superiority of the Romans by connecting them with great philosophers of the past. This brings us back again to the lineage that they were so proud of. Family, honor and shame, and wisdom, all worked in Paul's day to give a sense of belonging to those in the empire, unifying them and helping Rome to rule. These values defined the Corinthian identity which Paul needed to reshape for those who followed Christ.

Questions:

1. Who do you think of as part of your family? Have you ever included people in your family who weren't related to you?

2. How do we talk about people in ways that show respect? How do we shame people in our culture?

3. How do the three aspects of grace that Seneca talked about help you to envision God's grace?

4. What kind of a person does our culture consider wise, or maybe we would say smart?

FOLLOWERS OF CHRIST IN CORINTH

What happens when the people we have been discussing begin to follow Christ? Retired Roman soldiers, wealthy freedmen, women, merchants, servants, and slaves all assemble to worship God and to eat and celebrate the Lord's Supper together. We know a little bit about these early followers from the greetings Paul sends from Corinth at the end of his letter to the Romans.

Paul commends to them Phoebe from Cenchrea, the port to the east of Corinth. She probably carried Paul's letter to Rome, so she had enough money to be able to travel (Rom 16:1). Gaius had a living space large enough to host the whole assembly, and Erastus was a director of public works (1 Cor 1:14; Romans 16:23–24). Paul baptized both Gaius and Crispus whom Luke calls the synagogue leader (1 Cor 1:14; Acts 18:8). All four, then, must have had some wealth and standing in Corinth.

Stephanas is a bit more ambiguous. He has a Greek name, and yet he and his household are mentioned twice, and his travels and service to the community may indicate good financial status (1 Cor 1:16; 16:15–17).

Paul's reference to Chloe is also hard to analyze (1 Cor 1:11). He says he heard from her people, probably meaning her slaves. Although that implies that she had some wealth, Paul does not tell us whether she herself was a part of the Corinthian community.

Paul also sends greetings from Timothy, Lucius, Jason, Sosipater, Tertius (actually, he writes his own greeting), and Quartus (Rom 16:21–24). In 1 Corinthians itself, Paul names Achaicus and Fortunatus (1 Cor 16:17). There is little to go on in determining the social status of these men. Achaicus, Fortunatus, Quartus and Lucius (who is a Jew since Paul calls him his relative) have Latin names. In a Roman colony like Corinth, this could indicate that they were at least upwardly mobile. Tertius was a scribe, so for him we have a profession.

We have a few followers of Christ on the other end of the social scale. Chloe's people may have belonged to the community. In addition, Paul addresses slaves in his letter, and it seems reasonable to assume that he would only include this information if slaves would actually be among those listening (1 Cor 7:20–24).

We can collect some information from the topics that Paul covers, too. He advises the Corinthians to set aside some money at the beginning of every week (1 Cor 16:2). This implies that there were people with a small but variable income (or they could set aside a large sum immediately), like merchants or manual laborers. On the other hand, Paul wants to spend the winter in Corinth so they can help him on his way (1 Cor 16:6). This probably means supplying him with provisions for his journey; therefore some had the money to do that.

Probably, the best way to account for all of this data is to suppose that there were followers of Christ in Corinth in a range of income and status categories. Some people in the community had some wealth, some status, or both. Others may have been struggling for one or the other: Roman citizens trying to accumulate wealth or wealthy heads of households with the wrong background, the wrong gender, or no family name. The gathering also included people towards the lower end of the social scale.

We can use this information to see the way group identity could have created some of the conflicts Paul addressed. When followers of Christ moved in the circles of Corinth, in the law courts and when invited to dinners, their Roman Corinthian identity would rise to the top of their ladder (1 Cor 6; 10:27). If that identity stayed at the top when they entered the assembly, their behavior would conflict with the identity that Paul wanted them to develop in Christ. When they ate meals with other followers of Christ, those providing the meal may have expected to be honored in the usual Roman way. When they began baptizing new members of the community, the Roman behavior towards a patron at the baths might have caused followers of Christ to show loyalty and honor to the specific individual who baptized them. Paul writes to adjust these problems with their identity.

When persecuted, communities draw together and have little interaction with the surrounding culture. But in places like Corinth and in America, Christians and non-Christians interact daily. Followers of Christ do business in the city, and people from the outside attend worship (1 Cor 14:23–24). These situations create opportunities for sharing the gospel, but they can also confuse a group's identity. Starting in the next chapter, we will see the ways the background information from the first four chapters helps us understand Paul's concern for the Corinthians. From there, we can draw parallels to God's concern for us.

Questions:

1. How many different social, economic, educational, and cultural backgrounds are represented in your church?

2. How can we tell what class of people someone belongs to in our culture?

3. When do these differences work well together?

4. When do we allow them to create problems?

5

Who Are Followers of Christ?

1 Corinthians 1:1–9

> *Outside address: At the gymnasium. To Theon the son of Nikoboulos,
> the olive oil supplier.*
> *Indike to her lady Thaisous greeting. I sent the breadbasket to
> you by means of Taurinos, the camel driver; regarding which, please
> send word to me that you received it. Salute my lord Theon and
> Nikoboulos and Dioskopos and Theon and Hermokles, may all be
> free from harm. Longinus salutes you. Good-bye.*[1]
>
> *~ from the late first century, a letter from a woman to her mother,*
> *or from a servant to her mistress*

LETTER-WRITING STANDARDS HAVE CHANGED since the first century. In third grade, I learned that letters should have three parts: the greeting, the body, and the closing. This format is so important that most standard word processors have templates to help us follow it.

Within these rules, however, we have the freedom to improvise. *To Dr. John Brown* sounds much more formal than *dearest Cecilia*. At the end of a letter, *respectfully yours*, *your friend*, and *lots of love* express different levels of closeness in the relationship between the writer and the recipi-

---

1. White, *Letters*, 146. This is a fun book to look through, especially if you have ever been tempted to read someone else's mail. It lets you peek over the shoulders of some of the mothers and sons and soldiers and rulers who lived within about 300 years of Christ.

ent. We can tailor the letter to communicate the right intimacy for each situation.

The first century also had letter-writing standards. Most started with four pieces of information: the name of the writer, the name of the person being addressed, a greeting, and a prayer. If you are familiar with the New Testament, you probably recognize these elements from the beginnings of the letters there. First Corinthians is no exception.

LIVING IN LIGHT OF THE PAST: 1 CORINTIANS 1:1–6

Although Paul follows the letter-writing conventions of his day, he adapts them for his purposes. He starts by reminding the Corinthians of their past and of the group identity that should come from their common experience with God.

Paul identifies himself along with "our brother Sosthenes" as the letter writer. By including Sosthenes in his opening, Paul reduces any dominating tone that his audience might have otherwise heard. He shares leadership with others. We will see the way Paul moves back and forth in tone throughout the letter. He does have some authority in the community, and he insists on a hearing. But he wants to encourage, build up, and empower them, not dominate over them. So he sometimes reminds the Corinthians of his credentials, but he also puts himself on the same level.

Paul gives some of his credentials in the first verse: he is "called to be an apostle of Christ Jesus by the will of God" (1:1). Paul refers to God's call often in this letter. Here Paul remembers this past event because it gave him the position that he now holds, one that he did not choose for himself. He answered God's invitation in the same way that the Corinthians themselves did. In his case, however, he was called to be an apostle.

An apostle is like an ambassador. Although it is an important position, the one who holds it stands in for someone else. Paul is nothing in himself, but his actions are directed by God. This means that he is connected both to the Corinthians and to God. In this way he establishes himself as a model for group behavior.

Next, Paul identifies the people he is writing to. Again, he uses a letter-writing convention to point back to God's call, this time to the Corinthians. Paul is already shaping their identity. In the same way that

Paul's apostleship was from God, he is now writing "to the church of God in Corinth, to those sanctified in Christ Jesus and called to be holy" (1:2a).

When we talk about a call from God, sometimes Christians back each other into corners. Has anyone ever come up to you and announced, "I was called by God to tell you that you should . . ."? Even if the speaker has heard from God (and I am not discounting that possibility), this kind of opening leaves us with very little we can say except "Yes, sir," unless we want to question someone else's faith. Rather than being cornered, most of us would rather have some freedom to think about the call and evaluate it in light of our own understanding of God's will.

Paul gives the Corinthians just that freedom. He makes sure that they do not take him as their only authority. After all, the Corinthian followers of Christ were also called. Their community is privileged, but they are not independent. They all, Paul and the Corinthians, depend on God.

The Corinthians' calling means that they have been made holy (sanctified) and are also called to holiness. This double reference effectively includes both their present and their future. They should live now the way God has made them to be. Holiness has to be one of the values of their identity in Christ.

Paul specifies that this community is in Corinth, but he follows this up at the end of the verse by including among the people he is writing to "all those everywhere who call on the name of our Lord Jesus Christ— their Lord and ours" (1:2b). The Corinthian followers of Christ are not alone; God's call has made them not only dependent on God but also a part of a larger network.

Group commitment is affected by connections between a local group and any larger organization, such as a national or international establishment. Especially during a time of transition, leaders on a local level can refer to the larger group in order to strengthen the ties of their members. When leaders remind people of the values held by the organization, they communicate a sense of belonging that will carry people through any uncertainties they may feel about local change.

This relationship exists between any small group connected to a larger, more centralized, or more powerful group. The larger group sets the values and controls the resources, but also provides a legitimate reason for the smaller group to exist. This helps members feel confident and connected.

Paul often reminded the Corinthians about their connection to the Jerusalem community and, as here, to the followers of Christ around the Mediterranean. In this way, he made his hearers conscious of others who were also trying to live out an identity based in Christ. Without persecution, the followers of Christ in Corinth had kept too much of the surrounding culture in their identity. Paul tells them that because God has called them, they should value holiness like the other the followers of Christ around the Mediterranean do. This would gently pressure the Corinthians to become more unified and help them to adopt an identity based in Christ.

Paul next greets the Corinthian followers of Christ in a way that continues to reshape their identity: "Grace and peace to you from God our father and the Lord Jesus Christ" (1:3). Christians are familiar with the phrase *grace and peace* because Paul uses it in all of his letters, but it would not have been the greeting his listeners expected. By changing a few letters, Paul turned the Greek word for *greetings* into *grace* and then added the Hebrew greeting, *shalôm, peace*. This distinctive phrase that Paul seems to have invented greets both Jews and gentiles.

With these words, Paul separates the followers of Christ from the culture of Corinth. In the Roman Empire, the Emperor gave his grace to the nations in the form of the *Pax Romana*, the Roman peace. So when Paul points out that grace and peace for the Corinthians comes from God *our* father, he puts distance between them and their neighbors and friends in Corinth, and brings them into community with the followers of Christ around the world.

The final element of the letter opening, the prayer, continues to emphasize dependence on God and Christ. Paul prays, "I always thank God for you because of his grace given you in Christ Jesus. For in him you have been enriched in every way—in all your speaking and in all your knowledge—because our testimony about Christ was confirmed in you" (1:4–6). "So that you do not lack any gift of grace" (1:7a).[2] Paul prays for the whole community of followers of Christ. He thanks God for *them* because of his grace given to *them* in Christ Jesus. In him *they* have been enriched in every way because the testimony about Christ was confirmed in *them*, so that *they* do not lack any gift of grace. The plural *you* doesn't show up in our English translations, but we need to be sure we imagine

2. Verses 4–6 from the NIV. Verse 7a based on Tucker, *You Belong*, 146.

a messenger reading the letter to all of the people assembled together. Then, speaking to the community, he points back to its beginning. As the Corinthians remembered God's call, they remembered, too, the grace they received from God in the form of gifts, including the speech and knowledge they valued so much. Since they continue to receive gifts, they know that Christ's presence continues among them. Recognizing and re-membering these things strengthens their group identity in opposition to that of the Roman culture that surrounds them.

These elements of identity that Paul emphasizes right from the start of the letter can get forgotten in our culture, as well. He reminds us to balance the common calling of all with the specific calling of each of us. The rich gifts that we have in our communities, gifts that we will look at more closely below, show the reality of Christ. And because of that reality, we live in dependence on God rather than on anything—government, businesses, or education—that promises to take care of us.

Questions:

1. What are some of the roles that God has called people to in your community of followers of Christ?

2. When did you first hear God's call?

3. In what ways do you see your community valuing holiness?

4. Does your local Christian community belong to a larger organization? Are you connected to other Christians in any way?

LIVING IN LIGHT OF THE FUTURE: 1 CORINTIANS 1:7–9

If the witness of Christ was confirmed in us, then, like the Corinthians, we as a church family do not lack any gift of grace.[3] This is an astonishing statement! How many times have we looked around our churches and thought, "If only someone would take care of the nursery, lead the small group, fix the coffee." However, the logical conclusion from this verse, for people living in Christ, is that any project that we don't have the gifts to accomplish must not be on God's agenda for us at this time. This means

3. Tucker, *You Belong*, 146. NIV translates this as "spiritual gift," but I include as *gifts* anything that comes with each person God calls into our Christian community: miracu-lous abilities, natural talents, financial resources, and physical aptitudes.

that we have to both be willing to use the gifts that God has given us and to drop programs that God has not provided the resources for.

This kind of living requires constant dependence on God. That can sometimes be challenging if we care too much about what our church looks like to those outside. Dependence on God can look like weakness, inefficiency, or procrastination. Although our identity can include strength, efficiency, and action, they become problems if they are higher on the ladder than holiness and obedience to God's call. When we look at them as rungs on a ladder of identities, we escape an all-or-nothing mentality and put our values in balance.

The Corinthians probably would have heard this statement from an opposite perspective. They would have agreed with Paul, "Yep! We've got it all!" (1 Cor 4:8). Later in the letter, Paul will have something to say to them about that attitude.[4]

For now, he puts these gifts into perspective. He has reminded the Corinthians of the beginning of their community; now he points them towards its purpose: "So that you do not lack any gift of grace as you wait eagerly for the revelation of our Lord Jesus Christ" (1:7).[5] Followers of Christ live now in the presence of the future.

"He will keep you strong to the end, so that you will be blameless on the day of our Lord Jesus Christ" (1:8). God gives strength for today and righteousness for the end. These things are sure because "God . . . is faithful" (1:9). The gifts that we have today, including strength, show God's faithfulness, and that same faithfulness makes it certain that the Day of the Lord is really coming.

This coming revelation was well known in Judaism. Amos, Ezekiel, Joel, and Zephaniah warned the unrighteous not to long for the Day of the Lord since it would be a day of judgment for them (Amos 5:18–20; Ezek 30:1–4; Joel 2:1–2; Zeph 1:14–18). They called the people of Israel to repentance because God "is gracious and compassionate, slow to anger and abounding in love" (Joel 2:13). When the Day of the Lord comes, which Paul renames the Day of our Lord Jesus Christ, everything will be made right. Paul seems to assume, then, that the gentile followers of Christ would be familiar with the Jewish Scriptures. Paul needed to

4. See chapter 9.
5. Tucker, *You Belong*, 146.

ground them even more in the history of God among God's people as he tried to disconnect them from the world of Rome.

For a Jewish follower of Christ, the Scriptures would already have shaped their identity. The existence of one God who cares for his people, life after death, sin as disobedience to God, these concepts would always have been a part of one's mental furniture. David and Esther were role models, and words like *holiness*, *blamelessness*, and *revelation* were common vocabulary. If you grew up in the church, you may identify with that.

If you are like me, though, your early picture of reality was quite different. In my world, Christians were nice people, but a little foolish. God might exist, but how would we know? Even if he did, he probably wasn't interested in us. There was no life after death, or at least we couldn't know anything about it. We should try to be good people and find our own happiness. My family's values included education, intelligence, and looking good in society. When I became a Christian, I had to learn to live within a whole new framework.

That process begins at conversion, but it never really ends. No matter what environment shapes our early years, our understanding of life in Christ needs continuous reshaping. Paul is doing that here, reminding the Corinthian followers of Christ that their lives now should be lived out in the presence of Jesus who comes (in the past, present, and future) to set the world right according to God's standards.

Questions:

1. God's gifts show his faithfulness. How is your community using your gifts as you wait for Jesus' return?

2. How is God keeping you strong so that you will be blameless on the Day of the Lord Jesus Christ?

3. How does thinking about the Day of the Lord help you to evaluate who you should be today?

4. How has your view of life changed in your lifetime, maybe even recently, to line up more with God's view?

LIVING IN FELLOWSHIP: 1 CORINTHIANS 1:9

In this verse, Paul reminds the Corinthians again of the founding of the community by "God, who has called you into fellowship with his Son Jesus Christ our Lord" (1:9). This fellowship of God's Son has three important aspects.

The first seems minor to us because it is so familiar: Paul writes that Jesus is the Son of God. However, since the Roman Emperor was also called son of god, Paul is reminding the Corinthian followers of Christ that they do not worship or serve *him*. They have another Son of God as their master, Jesus Christ, risen from the dead, bringing resurrection to all, coming to rule over all (1 Cor 15:20–28). This separates the community in Christ from the people who live around them. They have a different Lord who gives them a different peace (1 Cor 1:3). Corinthians without faith in Christ should be their outgroup.

Second, we have once again a calling of a group of people into life in community. Paul used the word *church* in verse 2, a word meaning something like assembly, which in the first century simply meant a group of people who got together often for political or religious purposes. For Paul, it would have echoed the gathering of the people of Israel, as well. Paul's focus is on a community of people called to identify with each other.

Finally, this fellowship is based in Jesus Christ the Lord, who has invited his people to participate in his mission to the world until his return. Paul keeps bringing the Corinthians back to their call in this letter, and this call to mission will come up again in the next chapter. We see already, though, that Paul expects the Corinthian followers of Christ to be involved in mission just as he is. God's mission should be at the center of the identity of the community.

This kind of central purpose brings people together. They willingly give up some of their independence, some of their personal preferences, so that the goal can be accomplished. In a family, purposes might include providing food, building a common life, and nurturing children. At work, common goals include getting the job done, helping the company grow, building a team, or keeping the boss happy.

But what about our churches? Paul reminds the Corinthians that they have been called into just this kind of fellowship, called together for a common purpose. Later on in this letter, he writes more about the way he expects the followers of Christ to give themselves fully, to use their spiritual gifts, and to submit to those to whom God has given leadership (1 Cor 12:7–11; 15:58; 16:10, 15–16). As they share together in the experience of life with Christ, they work together to advance God's rule in the world. And for us, as we learn to use our individual gifts, we find the role that fits within God's mission and centers our identity in Christ.

I have a brass cross hanging on my wall that helps me picture this.[6] Its four arms are broad, all the same length, and covered with scenes. At the top, a dove holds an olive branch. Four people stand in a row beneath that, three of them hammering on an anvil and one fixing a wheel. The crosspiece is made up of a whole row of people: some holding books, some holding babies, an old person with a cane, a young person on a bike, a family, a teacher, children under a tree. Rows of people continue down the bottom arm: people sweeping and farming and caring for the sick, people digging and harvesting and cuddling children. All of these people, as they go about their daily lives, use the gifts and opportunities that God has given them. They work in the power of his Spirit, they form together the presence of Christ in the world, and they bring glory to God. This cross shows the people of God living their calling in Christ.

The emphasis on Jesus Christ, whom Paul names ten times in the first ten verses, continues into the next section of the letter as Paul begins to explain to the Corinthians what it means to be in Christ and what this community of God should look like.

Questions:

1. How much does your Christian community share life together?

2. How does your community fit into the purposes of God in the world?

3. How do the purposes of your community make you different from your neighbors?

4. How does your community cooperate with other followers of Christ to do the work of God in the world?

6. Created by Egino G. Weinert, the cross can be seen at http://www.eginoweinert.de/ by clicking on *Onlineshop* and searching for *Kreuz K31*.

6

Are Followers of Christ Respectable?

1 Corinthians 1:10–31

About fifty or sixty years ago, in a small town in Illinois, there lived a woman who could neither read nor write. She wanted to tell people about Jesus, so she would walk down Main Street and open the door of every store she came to. Sticking her head in, she would call out, "Everybody happy in here? You can be if you love Jesus!" Embarrassing? Perhaps. But when she died, all the local business owners came to her funeral.

~contributed by Darold Hill

I stood outside the library, waiting for it to open. Another woman came to join me at the door. We exchanged smiles, then hellos. She sighed, "Sometimes, I just don't know what it's all about."

I kept the smile on my face, but my mind scrambled. Help! This is a witnessing opportunity! What should I say? I forced myself to ask her, "Do you mean what is life all about?" "Yes," she said.

Oh, no! I should tell her about Jesus! But how do I start? People aren't supposed to talk about Jesus in public to strangers! I don't want to sound like a religious nut! I was still standing there trying to come up with a coherent reply when the library doors opened. The moment was gone.

~Laura

WHEN PEOPLE DON'T EXPERIENCE persecution, they blend in with their culture. They want to be accepted. They don't want to look like fools. Yet we know that God has called us. So how do we focus on God's mission when our values get in the way, the values of the very identity that helps us to interact with other people every day?

COMPETITION VERSUS MISSION: 1 CORINTHIANS 1:10–17

Earlier in the letter Paul had connected the community with "those everywhere who call on the name of the Lord Jesus Christ" (1 Cor 1:2). Paul starts this section by calling on that name himself. "I appeal to you, brothers, in the name of our Lord Jesus Christ, that all of you agree with one another so that there may be no divisions among you and that you may be perfectly united in mind and thought" (1:10). So Paul begins right away to reset their identities, shifting the Corinthians' allegiance to Jesus to the top of the ladder. In Christ's name, Paul calls them to unity of mind and thought.

Now, this does not mean that Paul expects everyone to act and think exactly the same. He knows, for example, that their community includes married, single, and divorced people, so that having the same mind does not mean that everyone makes the same choices (1 Cor 7:8–15, 27–28, 36–38). Paul's idea of unity, then, assumes diversity, as well. How can this work?

Paul explains by painting some shocking pictures for the Corinthians of what this diversity is *not*. "My brothers, some from Chloe's household have informed me that there are quarrels among you. What I mean is this: One of you says, 'I follow Paul'; another, 'I follow Apollos'; another, 'I follow Cephas'; still another, 'I follow Christ.' Is Christ divided? Was Paul crucified for you? Were you baptized into the name of Paul?" (1:11–13).

Christ, broken up into little pieces, each one claimed by a different group? Leaders, each crucified for a small band of followers baptized in the leader's name? These pictures contrast dramatically with the truth: Members of the community do not own pieces of Christ; instead *they* belong to *him* (1 Cor 3:23). No leader was crucified except Christ. No one baptizes in anyone's name but Christ's. By startling them with these descriptions, Paul begins to break the strength of their identification within their divisions. He then seems to take a detour into a discussion about baptism. However, maybe baptism combined with Roman culture was contributing to the divisions in the first place.

We saw in chapter 4 the way clients competed for patrons in the Roman Empire. Bathing practices were tied to those relationships. Patrons might pay to build a new bathhouse or cover the cost of the baths during a specific period of time. Clients met with their patrons at the baths. A patron surrounded by lots of clients had more honor than someone surrounded by only a few. And a client of a more honored patron had more honor himself. This way of dividing up honor would also divide the upper levels of society into followers of one patron or another.

This system may also have caused competition to develop in the community. Each baptism would create a group of people loyal to the baptizer. The usual practice of bringing honor to one's patron would extend into the kind of boasting that was a normal part of the client's responsibility. Maybe that's why Paul continues by writing, "I am thankful that I did not baptize any of you except Crispus and Gaius, so no one can say that you were baptized into my name" (1:14–15). In Corinth, maybe the person who baptized you became your patron.

Stephanas's case extends the problem from an individual to a household. "Yes, I also baptized the household of Stephanas; beyond that, I don't remember if I baptized anyone else" (1:16). The Roman sense of family extended to all who lived together: slaves, servants, and relatives. Household loyalties, then, might create separations in the community, especially if the groups met in homes for worship. Members of Stephanas's household, already proud of their connection to an important leader of the community, would now have the added honor of participating in the assembly that met at his house.

Baptism could add to that sense of belonging. One of Gaius's slaves, for example, might see herself as owned by Gaius, baptized by Gaius, and part of the group meeting for worship at Gaius's house. This makes for a strong attachment to him! If he disagreed with Stephanas even about something small, she might feel the need to stand up for him in conversations with other slaves. Even if Gaius and Stephanas thought of themselves as brothers and got along well, this heightened sense of belonging could have caused the followers of Christ in Corinth to line up behind their favorite leader in a competition for honor.

So followers themselves can create the kinds of divisions we are talking about, but leaders can play the game, too. Baptism would give you your own group of people ready to take your side in every conflict, maybe even dependent on your gifts for support. Baptismal ceremonies would shift away from focusing on the good news of Christ towards the promotion of a patron.

Of course, Paul himself had baptized several of the Corinthian leaders. In their thinking, this would make him their patron and give him some authority over them. His reminder about their baptisms may subtly call them to pay attention, but he then shows them a different kind of leadership.

First, Paul corrects the leaders indirectly. Although he names local leaders in connection with his baptisms, he names himself, Apollos, Peter, and Jesus when he lists the leaders of the divided groups. He later writes, "I have applied these things to myself and Apollos for your benefit," so he may have substituted his own name and the names of other well-known men to avoid embarrassing the local leaders—possibly even Crispus, Gaius, and Stephanas (1 Cor 4:6). This is especially likely since none of the leaders Paul does mention were in Corinth at the time he was writing.[1] Paul shows the Corinthian leaders the problems with their divisions but without embarrassing them by shaming them publicly. It's as though a pastor told his congregation, "You keep arguing over whose sermons are best, but none of the leaders you're listening to, including me, were crucified for you." He not only wants them to stop fighting about national Christian speakers but about their small group leaders, as well.

Paul also models good leadership by calling his listeners *brothers* (1 Cor 1:10–11). This both puts them in the same family and sets him as their equal. Although he encourages them and even gives them direction, he doesn't order them around. He later asks them to imitate him, so he expects the leaders to do what he does: to avoid shaming others and to see themselves as members of the community (1 Cor 4:16).

Paul continues to use himself as an example as he reminds the Corinthians of the importance of God's mission: "For Christ did not send me to baptize, but to preach the gospel—not with words of human wisdom, lest the cross of Christ be emptied of its power" (1:17).

---

1. Paul was obviously not there. Apollos was a native of Alexandria (Acts 18:24) and traveled quite a bit (to Ephesus in Acts 18:24, to Crete in Titus 3:13). He did spend time in Corinth, but he wasn't there when Paul wrote this letter (Acts 19:1; 1 Cor 16:12). The book of Acts shows Peter traveling, too, but never mentions him in Corinth, so it's unlikely that he was directly involved in the divided groups. Finally, Jesus was present by means of the Spirit, but he was certainly not competing with other leaders (1 Cor 2:16)!

This verse wraps up this topic in the strongest way possible. The NIV uses "preach the gospel," which may bring to mind pulpits, sermons or old-time revival meetings, but the Greek word could be translated "tell the good news." It includes talking about God's call through Jesus in any setting (even while waiting for the library to open). Preaching the gospel—telling the good news—comes first. Paul reminds the Corinthians that those were his priorities, and since he is one of the models for the community, he expects to be imitated. He does not want the Corinthians to stop baptizing, but he does want them to find a better balance. They should refocus their attention on Christ, not on who baptized whom.

We might think that since our culture does not include patrons, clients, and large households, we don't have these kinds of tensions. But as we look at the groups we do belong to, we see the same sorts of competitions going on. Sports teams compete for fans. Authors compete for sales. Churches compete for members. Belonging to these different groups *does* help us to identify who we are. As we saw in an earlier chapter, we define ourselves in part by telling ourselves who we are not. We compare leaders, and we like ours best. This kind of positioning strengthens our identity and can therefore help members commit themselves to group values. In this sense, it's a good thing.

But when a person's connection to the group becomes more important than identification with Christ, differences become divisions. A church where each small group chooses its own name and symbol may simply be encouraging healthy group identity formation. However, sometimes groups define themselves in opposition to everyone else. I once belonged to a small group that prided itself on never going along with anything the church leadership wanted us to do. In private, we called ourselves "The Rebels" but the name of our small group was Agape. Our identity was definitely in conflict with what we said we believed. We were over-identifying with our group and making the rest of the church into our outgroup. We had lost our connection to the greater church community.

People also compete over their callings and gifts. The praise band has more status than the hospitality team. The head of evangelism seems more important than the small group leader. The pastor secretly wishes he had the same honor as the missionaries. Each church member believes that she belongs to the best (defined as the largest, the most intellectual, the most relevant, or the most practical) denomination, class, or small group. We use clothes and vocabulary to compete with each other and to establish who is 'in' and who is 'out.' We stake out our territory and establish our little kingdoms. If you know our Christian jargon and dress like we do (whether suits or jeans) you are definitely one of us. We use the values of our culture (biggest, most expensive, coolest, newest, techiest) to evaluate church programs.

Our identification with the culture includes, as we saw with Stephanas, identification with our families, as well. Although some of us have little connection with extended family, others feel pressure from relatives who expect that our commitment to them will always trump our loyalty to our church. On any given night, God could call us to minister to the youth *or* to our family, but we may have trouble hearing his leading when the voices of both groups are sounding in our ears.

Membership in various groups within and outside of the church pull at us as they pulled at the Corinthians. Baptism, though important, had begun to feed their desire for social status. Paul calls them to refocus their thoughts and change their behavior. Instead of leaders who seek honor by baptism and followers who gain honor by claiming loyalty to the most important leaders, Paul wants his hearers to understand the central place and unifying power of the good news.

Questions:

1. What are the different circles in your church community?

2. Are they just different, or are they divided?

3. What identities sometimes come before our identification with Christ?

4. How could we become less preoccupied with how well we fit in?

RESPECTABILITY VERSUS FOOLISHNESS: 1 CORINTHIANS 1:18—2:5

We have wise sayings in America: "Don't count your chickens before they hatch." "The early bird gets the worm." We read self-help books and watch television talk shows that shape our ideas about the right way to live. We believe in education to get a good job. We believe exercise and a good diet lead to good health. We encourage individual achievement but also a concern for others. Another word for respectability and wisdom might just be *smart*. Smart people get ahead.

We not only have our ideas of wisdom, but our society values power, as well. When my daughter was a toddler, her older brothers were talking about what they wanted to be when they grew up. One of them turned to her and asked, "Beth, what do *you* want to be?" Without hesitation, she answered, "The boss!" Adults may phrase things more tactfully, yet secretly feel the same way. A company manager had an employee that he valued. He promoted him, gave him the best assignments, offered him travel and other perks. He then commented, "I have now done him so many favors that I *own* him." Even kindness can be used to gain power.

Of course, wisdom and power go together, really. If we're smart, we will act wisely and that will bring us power, at least over our own circumstances if not over others. This smart thinking goes on inside as well as outside our churches. This may be caused in part by a lack of persecution. If *they* are trying to kill us just because we exist, we worry less about fitting in with *them*. We have less contact with *them* and *their* ideas don't influence us as much. But without clear boundaries between *us* and *them* we fit into society and adopt its standards. This means that we can have a voice there for mission, but it also means that we bring society's ideas about respectability into the church. We may look just like the rest of our culture, with a few added ceremonies and rituals thrown in. Christianity can then become one more piece of wisdom that we use to build ourselves a respectable life with the Bible as our self-help book and Jesus as another advice columnist.

This problem was infecting the Corinthian community. They, like us, could move in and out of various circles in their world. Those people valued wisdom. Dio Chrysostom, a Greek living in the Roman Empire in the first century, wrote, "This alone I consider useful to have—to know those who are wise, and also powerful and understand everything."[2] Virgil in the *Aeneid* wrote, "Fortune aids the daring."[3] That sounds a lot like "God helps those who help themselves."

Power, too, was important to the Romans. Those with good family names could move up into government positions, especially with money behind them. The patron-client system allowed patrons to increase their importance by giving out favors. The clients who accepted those favors could be relied on for support in elections. Of course, clients benefited,

2. Dio Chrysostom, *Discourses* 12.10.

3. Virgil, *Aeneid* 10.284.

too. They might get access to the court systems which they wouldn't otherwise have. Even advice from the wise became an exchange of power. In Corinth, this was just the way things were done. Paul tries to correct this problem. "God," he says, "has turned all of this upside down."

A Foolish Message: 1 Cor 1:18–25

Paul tells the Corinthian followers of Christ that "the message of the cross is foolishness to those who are perishing, but to us who are being saved it is the power of God" (1:18). What the world considered respectable, God has shown to be foolishness, and what looks so foolish—the message about a savior who suffered—God has shown to be wise.

God had done this sort of thing before. He said to Isaiah, "These people come near to me with their mouth and honor me with their lips, but their hearts are far from me. Their worship of me is made up only of rules taught by men. Therefore once more I will astound these people with wonder upon wonder; the wisdom of the wise will perish, the intelligence of the intelligent will vanish" (Isa 29:13–14). In the past, too, when religious observances became infected with the way to get ahead and God's people lost God's heart for the humble and the needy, God turned their understanding of wisdom and intelligence upside down (Isa 29:19). Paul quotes a part of this passage for the Corinthians, "For it is written: 'I will destroy the wisdom of the wise; the intelligence of the intelligent I will frustrate'" (1:19).

The Corinthians want wisdom, but Paul asks, "Where is the wise man? Where is the scholar? Where is the philosopher of this age?" (1:20a). We might look at our church communities and ask similar questions. Where is the millionaire? Where is the talk show host? Where is the news anchor? The kind of wisdom necessary for those jobs does not usually lead to the knowledge of God. He has made that wisdom foolish, and instead, has used foolishness to save those who believe. This foolish message alone contains true wisdom and power.

Paul goes on, "Has not God made foolish the wisdom of the world? For since in the wisdom of God the world through its wisdom did not know him, God was pleased through the foolishness of what was preached to save those who believe" (1:20b–21). Followers of Christ need to be okay with foolishness. What we do and what we say won't always make sense to everybody else. We won't always look reasonable. After all, the message itself doesn't sound very smart. To the Roman world, a God who became a man and died a criminal's death sounded ridiculous. Christ's crucifixion was not exactly what the people of that day were looking for. "Jews demand miraculous signs and Greeks look for wisdom, but we preach Christ crucified: a stumbling block to Jews and foolishness to Gentiles, but to those whom God has called, both Jews and Greeks, Christ the power of God and the wisdom of God" (1:22–24). In our world, accepting a message that others reject is not popular either. And yet this message contains God's power, "For the foolishness of God is wiser than man's wisdom, and the weakness of God is stronger than man's strength" (1:25). It looks like foolishness, though.

I was raised with this assumption. In a household that valued higher education, Christianity looked stupid. When I was 17, my parents were getting divorced, and I shared my pain with my boyfriend's mother, Carole. She started talking about Jesus. "What?" I remember thinking. "Didn't you hear me? My parents are getting a divorce! What does Jesus have to do with that?" But as Carole continued to talk, I felt God's presence. Jesus walked into the room. God's power was displayed in that ordinary living room in West Virginia. The foolishness of what was preached once again saved someone who believed.

Questions:

1. Who are the respectable people both within and outside the church?

2. What does respectable behavior look like?

3. What parts of the good news about Jesus sound foolish?

4. Among which group of people outside the church is it hardest for you to talk about Jesus?

Foolish People: 1 Cor 1:26–31

Beyond the foolish message, we have foolish people, as well. Paul points out that God has also turned the Corinthians' status upside down.[4] He

---

4. For further information on status indicators in Corinth, interested readers may want to consult Friesen, "Demography."

tells his listeners, "Think of what you were when you were called," and apparently for most this was not a pretty picture. "Not many of you were wise by human standards, not many were influential; not many were of noble birth" (1:26). No one had any reason to think much of them yet God chose them, but not for any merit of their own. He chose them for the very reason that they were foolish, weak, lowly, despised nothings (1 Cor 1:27–28). This is embarrassing! These people are feeling fairly respectable, and Paul reminds them that when God called them, they were nothing. It's a good thing that Paul softens his words to them by calling them "brothers." He knew that he was no different.

God specializes in finding outcasts and redeeming them, after all. As individuals some of us may have wealth or power in the world, but as a whole, not many of us come from high society. In general, if you're looking for the doctors and the lawyers and the beautiful people, you don't look in the church. If you're looking for the ex-addicts, the ex-convicts, and the ex-failures, this is exactly where you come.

Once we joined the church, though, all of that changed. We got cleaned up on the inside, and we also changed on the outside. We learned the praise songs and the Christian jargon. We became choir directors and Sunday School teachers and building administrators. We began to acquire a reputation of wisdom and to enjoy the benefits of some power within our communities. We became respectable, and now our choices are sometimes designed to uphold that respectability rather than to obey the call of God. So this reminder from Paul about the Corinthians' circumstances when God called them can make us squirm, as well. The message seems foolish, and so do the people God chose.

Paul points out that God chose both Jews and Greeks. Our churches, as well, include people with all kinds of backgrounds. These differences don't go away when we walk inside. We are men and women, married and single and divorced. We eat fast food, gourmet food, Chinese, Italian, and Mexican. We vote Republican and Democrat and Independent. We read comic books, academic texts, romance novels, and Christian self-help. We have circles where we belong and circles where we don't. Still God has called all of us through the good news of Christ crucified.

We are the ones chosen by God. "But God chose the foolish things of the world to shame the wise; God chose the weak things of the world to shame the strong. He chose the lowly things of this world and the despised things—and the things that are not—to nullify the things that are, so that no one may boast before him" (1:27–29). We were not among the wise, but that's okay because God chose the foolish, and now we have righteousness in Christ Jesus. We were not among the powerful, but that's okay because God chose the weak, and now we have holiness in Christ Jesus. We were not nobly born, but that's okay because God chose the lowly, and now we have redemption in Christ Jesus. "It is because of him that you are in Christ Jesus, who has become for us wisdom from God— that is, our righteousness, holiness and redemption" (1:30). In Christ Jesus is found wisdom—but this time God's wisdom, a better wisdom than any of us were looking for. His righteousness, holiness, and redemption are better than any power we could have gotten with our own wisdom.

We are those who are being saved, those who believe, those who tell the good news of Christ crucified, those whom God has called. Although we have differences, we are called together and can use our differences to build bridges to those outside our church communities. They, too, are men and women, married and single and divorced. They eat fast food, gourmet food, Chinese, Italian, and Mexican. They vote Republican and Democrat and Independent. They read comic books, academic texts, ro- mance novels, and self-help books.

The fact that the followers of Christ in Corinth included men and women, Jews and gentiles, slaves and free meant that they could connect with those outside their community, as well. Paul calls those others on the outside "those who are perishing" (1 Cor 1:18). Now, if they had been persecuting the Corinthians, the followers of Christ might think, "Good! Let 'em perish! Go get 'em, God!" But since they are friends, neighbors, coworkers, and relatives, the Corinthians' response is quite different: "How can they be saved?"

Paul answers them in the next verse: by boasting about God. The change in those who are following Christ came about because of God, and therefore the Corinthians can boast, but not in their own wisdom or power (1 Cor 1:30). Instead, going back to Jeremiah, Paul writes, "Therefore, as it is written: 'Let him who boasts boast in the Lord'" (1:31).

In Jeremiah 9:23–24, we find again this same reversal of human ex- pectations. The prophet announces the coming destruction, the failure of the nation to save themselves by their own wisdom and power. Jeremiah says, "Let not the wise man boast of his wisdom or the strong man boast of his strength or the rich man boast of his riches, but let him who boasts boast about this: that he understands and knows me, that I am the LORD, who exercises kindness, justice and righteousness on earth, for in these I delight." That, in fact, is exactly what Paul wants the Corinthians to say: "I know God. He is the Lord, and he cares about kindness, justice, and righteousness. Let me tell you about him." That is preaching the gospel, telling the good news.[5]

Questions:

1. Were you a respectable person when God called you? Are you respectable now?

1. What would you say if you were going to boast about God?

3. How might God be calling you to boast about him to people outside the Christian community?

4. How might God be asking you to be foolish for the sake of talking about Jesus?

---

5. Bill Hybels and Mark Mittelberg give descriptions of the ways different personalities can live the gospel including confrontational, intellectual, testimonial, interpersonal, invitational, and service approaches. Hybels and Mittelberg, *Contagious*, 123–31. In addition, living the gospel includes a willingness to make daily decisions based on God's mission, with the wisdom given to us by God's Spirit, even if that makes us different.

7

Are Followers of Christ Mature?

1 Corinthians 2:1—3:4

Nadia carefully adjusted her scarf and walked across the mosque parking lot. "What would my church friends think?" she wondered. Still, her brother had asked her to emcee his wedding reception. All the women in their hijabs would watch the ceremony from the second floor balcony, and she would have to join them. After much prayer and a conversation with Pastor Joe, she had decided to wear a scarf over her head in the mosque. Then she could take it off to emcee. After all, she thought, head coverings aren't unbiblical! That seemed the best way, as a Christian, to negotiate her brother's Muslim wedding.

As she walked across the parking lot, she chuckled suddenly as she remembered the day last week when she had grabbed a scarf on the way out the door as protection against the cold. She had caught looks from several strangers that day, curious glances tinged with just a shade of suspicion—all because she was trying to keep warm!

"I guess," she decided, "a scarf is just a scarf. Staying connected to my family so that I can continue to live in Christ before them—that's what's important."

~from an interview with Nadia

THIS STORY SEEMS VERY distant from 1 Corinthians. After all, the people who heard Paul's letter were not interacting with Muslim culture, since Islam didn't exist then. But the Corinthian followers of Christ did have to figure out what their own community should look like while they kept their ties to people without faith in Christ. We have that same dilemma. We have to figure out what our church communities should look like while still keeping our ties with those in our neighborhoods, jobs, and families, no matter what their religious beliefs or cultural backgrounds are.

THE TYPE TO AVOID: 1 CORINTHIANS 2:1-10

In this section, Paul offers himself as a model and then contrasts himself with a stereotype of the people that he wants the Corinthian followers of Christ to see as their outgroup: Roman rulers. Paul starts by taking them back to the founding of their community. When we do this, when we tell stories about our beginnings, we connect the members to the original identity of the group. We remind ourselves and others about the reasons we belong.[1]

When Dr. Mayhew told us the story of the way God provided a library for Michigan Theological Seminary, in part through the odd hoarding habits of a man the founders didn't even know, I was glad to belong to an institution begun by the power of God. The story reinforced our identity as students of that particular seminary. By referring to the words he spoke at the beginning of their community, Paul reminds the Corinthians of their own original call. They, too, would feel a renewed sense of connection.

At the same time, he illustrates what he has been telling them about wisdom and power by offering himself as a model of the behavior he wants them to imitate. He does not say these things from a position of authority, though; he calls them brothers: "When I came to you, brothers, I did not come with eloquence or superior wisdom as I proclaimed to you the testimony about God" (2:1). Since Paul did not rely on the Greek wisdom that the Romans would value, neither should Corinthian followers of Christ. Instead, "I resolved to know nothing while I was with you except Jesus Christ and him crucified" (2:2). We saw in the last chapter that this message would have looked foolish to the Corinthians. Paul is basically telling them, "I came to you, and I was willing to look stupid!"

Furthermore, rather than relying on Roman power, Paul says, "I came to you in weakness and fear, and with much trembling" (2:3). Paul

---

1. For more information on memory and character development see Williams, "Abraham," 209–12.

lets them in behind the scenes and tells them that in his first visit to them, he had relied on the same power and wisdom he is now pointing them towards. Since Paul is a model for the identity in Christ that he wants for the Corinthians, they should rely on this same power and wisdom for their behavior.

Now Paul defines this new kind of wisdom and power. "My message and my preaching were not with wise and persuasive words, but with a demonstration of the Spirit's power, so that your faith might not rest on men's wisdom, but on God's power" (2:4–5). If the Corinthians saw any power in Paul's words, then it had to have come from the Spirit. Their faith had to rest on the power of God. If followers of Christ will turn away from trusting in human ideas of power, there is another kind of power available to them, that of the Spirit. Furthermore Paul says, "We do, however, speak a message of wisdom among the mature" (2:6a). Not only do followers of Christ have access to God's power, but Paul will show them that wisdom is available to them as well, if they are mature. The idea of maturity will become key as Paul moves forward.

Before telling them exactly what that wisdom looks like, though, he shows them the typical Roman ruler, the respectable person that they have been imitating and who, instead, should be a part of their outgroup. He says that the wisdom God provides is "not the wisdom of this age or of the rulers of this age, who are coming to nothing" (2:6b).

Have you ever watched someone with money and fame lose everything? In politics, entertainment, or religion, the news lets us know when a superstar falls. Paul predicts the same fate for the stars of his world. They had honor and wisdom, but not like Paul's. Therefore, the Corinthians should not imitate a wise, powerful Roman leader. We should not imitate the leaders in our society, either. Instead, we have to find God's kind of wisdom.

This wisdom is destined for our glory. "No, we speak of God's secret wisdom, a wisdom that has been hidden and that God destined for our glory before time began" (2:7). The Romans put great stock in destiny. Virgil's *Aeneid* gave shape to their sense that the gods had planned for the Roman Empire. The Romans were destined for the glory of ruling the world. Americans, too, have had a sense of manifest destiny. At one point in our history, we believed that God intended for us to rule "from sea to shining sea." But Paul is writing about a different destiny.

A Roman using Roman wisdom would seek Roman glory, but God's wisdom gives his people eternal glory. A Roman following Roman wisdom would fulfill the Roman destiny, but a follower of Christ has a God-ordained destiny. A Roman with only Roman wisdom would not even be able to make sense of God's plan. "None of the rulers of this age understood it, for if they had, they would not have crucified the Lord of glory" (2:8). Paul has taken the Roman ruler, and he has shown that he is not a good model for followers of Christ. Someone who can't recognize God's plan, who in fact would actively oppose God's plan, is not a person to imitate.

This idea—that people who don't follow God are not good role models for us—is echoed in other parts of the Bible, as well. Psalm 73 especially examines the fate of those who seem successful, whom the psalmist envies. He even begins to wonder if staying innocent and pure is pointless. But then he says, "I entered the sanctuary of God; then I understood their final destiny. Surely you place them on slippery ground; you cast them down to ruin" (Ps 73:17–18).

Psalm 37:1–4 describes a similar picture, "Do not fret because of evil men or be envious of those who do wrong; for like the grass they will soon wither, like green plants they will soon die away." At this point, though, they seem to be flourishing. But following God's ways produces different results: "Trust in the LORD and do good; dwell in the land and enjoy safe pasture. Delight yourself in the LORD and he will give you the desires of your heart."

Truly smart behavior, according to Paul, doesn't come from imitating those who seem to succeed in the world, those who look respectable. Paul even says that listening to our senses, the normal channels through which we get and process information, won't tell us what we need to know. His next words are a quotation shaped from Isaiah 64:4 and other similar ancient sayings: "However, as it is written: 'No eye has seen, no ear has heard, no mind has conceived what God has prepared for those who love him'" (2:9). Nobody could know what God was going to do for his people when they were relying on what they could see with their eyes, hear with their ears, and figure out in their minds. "But God has revealed it to us by his Spirit" (2:10a). Paul has shown the Corinthian followers of Christ the inadequacy of their previous role models. He replaces them with a person who has the Spirit of God.

So, when we look around our world, who are the smart ones? The rich, the famous, the stars? That's not what it takes to have God's kind of wisdom. It takes God's Spirit to get that.

Questions:

1. Who are the current stars in politics, entertainment, and business?

2. How do those people show that they don't have God's kind of wisdom?

3. How do we sometimes imitate them in our Christian communities?

4. What are some ways we could avoid this?

THE MODEL TO FOLLOW: 1 CORINTHIANS 2:10-16

Where do we get the wisdom we need to make good decisions? I've noticed that many Christian books, despite the variety of principles they offer, start the same way. Jim Cymbala told the congregation of The Brooklyn Tabernacle, "Brothers and sisters, I really feel that I've heard from God about the future of our church."[2] Rick Warren of Saddleback felt God's calling on his life as a pastor, felt God directing him to discover principles for growth, and heard God speaking clearly to him about where to start a new church.[3] Richard Stearns shows in the first three chapters of his book, *The Hole in our Gospel,* the way God cornered him into becoming the president of World Vision.[4] Each starts with the same basic statement, *I prayed; God said.* The rest of the book explains what happened as a result. But it seems to me that the most important information is in those first few pages: *I prayed, and God said.*

Nadia, for example, had to decide what to do when her brother invited her to come to his wedding and emcee the reception. If she detached herself completely from her Muslim family, they would no longer have the opportunity to see Christ in her. If she went back to acting just like a Muslim, she would no longer be living in Christ at all. Her decision had

2. Cymbala and Merrill, *Fresh,* 27.

3. Warren, *Purpose,* 26, 30, 34.

4. Stearns, *Hole,* 15–50.

to fall somewhere between these two extremes, and to find it she had to rely on the Holy Spirit. But what does the Spirit do?

Paul tells us that the Holy Spirit knows God's thoughts and therefore God's wisdom. "The Spirit searches all things, even the deep things of God. For who among men knows the thoughts of a man except the man's spirit within him? In the same way no one knows the thoughts of God except the Spirit of God" (2:10b–11). So the only way to know God's wisdom is to have God's Spirit.

That is exactly what Paul says that people living in Christ have: "We have not received the spirit of the world but the Spirit who is from God, that we may understand what God has freely given us. This is what we speak, not in words taught us by human wisdom but in words taught by the Spirit, expressing spiritual truths in spiritual words" (2:12–13). Paul and the others who teach in the community rely on God's Spirit who gives them the wisdom to know what to say. However, the Spirit not only *expresses*, as the NIV translates, but even better *discerns*. This wisdom of the Spirit teaches Paul to evaluate correctly, as well.

This wisdom operates differently from the wisdom of the Roman rulers. Whereas Roman rule depended on military power enforced externally, God's Spirit gives God's wisdom on the inside. The Spirit communicates the thoughts of God.

Paul then explains the purpose of God's Spirit: to make correct judgments. He contrasts again the typical person of the outgroup with the model for the followers of Christ. "The man without the Spirit does not accept the things that come from the Spirit of God, for they are foolishness to him, and he cannot understand them, because they are spiritually discerned. The spiritual man makes judgments about all things, but he himself is not subject to any man's judgment" (2:14–15). The Roman thinks that Jesus and the cross are foolish. They do not match his ideas of wisdom and power. He can't understand them and so rejects them. His judgments, therefore, are not the ones to accept. On the contrary, the model for a follower of Christ should be the spiritual person. This is someone who judges accurately by God's Spirit and cannot be judged by outsiders or those using an outsider's standards. Nadia knew that not everyone would agree with her decision, but she felt confident in God's approval. Furthermore, and we will see in the next two chapters the importance of this, wearing a scarf to the mosque fit best with her mission in Christ.

So how does this work in practice? Paul and his companions apparently knew what the Spirit was telling them, but how do we know today? I have to admit that it is hard for me to even ask this question, but Paul won't let me wriggle out of it. He clearly tells the Corinthian followers of Christ that the only way to have God's kind of wisdom and power is to listen to God's Spirit, which God has freely given. But have you ever tried to listen to God's Spirit? Have you heard the cacophony of voices clamoring inside our heads?

It seems to me that we tend to react to that confusion in two different ways. On the one hand, we decide that listening to voices is just crazy. So we step away from that scary place, and we go back to making decisions with our eyes, our ears, and our minds. We give up the access that we have to God's mind because it is just too hard to figure out what he is saying. We rationalize God's wisdom right out of existence using the wisdom of the world.

If we are determined, though, to hear God's Spirit, we can go in the other direction. Out of a sincere desire to hear and follow God, we may decide that *every* voice in our head must be God's voice. We passionately want to do anything he asks us to do, we are completely willing to look foolish to the world around us for the sake of Christ, but we are not sure which voice is his. So we obey them all!

In between these two extremes, Paul gives direction that can help. For one thing, Paul is talking to the community as a whole. He says that God has revealed his plans to *us* by his Spirit and that *we* have not received the spirit of the world but the Spirit who is from God so that *we* may understand what God has freely given *us*. This gift has been given to the community, and listening to others can help us sort through the voices.

The body of Christ, in fact, is bigger than our local gathering. In the first section of this letter, we saw the way Paul reminded the Corinthians that they had connections to other brothers and sisters around the Mediterranean. We, too, have connections not only around the world but also through the centuries. When we hear the insights of Christians in Korea, when we read Christian writers from the last 2000 years, we find God's wisdom, given by his Spirit, expressed by his people in various circumstances. Looking for God's wisdom in others helps us to hear his Spirit in ways that alone we might miss. It also makes us value each other. If God may be speaking to me through you, I had better be listening!

In our search for God's wisdom, Paul asks the same question we are asking: "For who has known the mind of the Lord that he may instruct him?" (2:16a). When Isaiah asked this question, the implied answer was "no one" (Isa 40:13). No one has the power or the gentleness or the knowledge or the wisdom that God has (Isa 40:10–14). Now, however, "we have the mind of Christ" (2:16b). As we value each other in our community promoting the unity of mind and thought that Paul asked for at the beginning of his letter, we have access to God's wisdom through the gift of his Spirit.

Questions:

1. When have your plans clearly been guided by the Holy Spirit?

2. Have you ever realized that plans that seemed great on paper were not what God wanted you to do?

3. How have others, either in your local church or in the worldwide church through the centuries, helped you to understand God's plans for you a little better?

4. How would listening for the Spirit, and looking for the mind of Christ in community help you to make decisions according to the wisdom of God?

THE MATURITY TO HEAR: 1 CORINTHIANS 3:1–4

Paul has offered himself as a model in contrast to the Roman ruler. He has pointed out the way followers of Christ have access to the Holy Spirit who communicates God's wisdom. He has been helping the Corinthian followers of Christ to see the ways they needed to be different from the rest of the Corinthians. He has described the problems of not having access to God's Spirit and contrasted that with the benefits the Spirit provides. In this way, he has created a model for the community. Now, Paul sets up another comparison. He contrasts an infant with a mature person. This discussion of maturity can also help us to distinguish the voice of God's Spirit.

Paul starts by going back again to their beginning. "Brothers, I could not address you as spiritual but as worldly—mere infants in Christ. I gave you milk, not solid food, for you were not yet ready for it" (3:1–2a).

Beginning information was appropriate for beginning followers of Christ, but Paul continues, "Indeed, you are still not ready. You are still worldly" (3:2b–3a).

Have you ever been called a baby—told you weren't old enough to do something? How did you react? If you're like me, you straightened up tall, threw your shoulders back and your chin out, and said, "I am, too, old enough!"—and then you tried to prove it by behaving in a more grown-up way. Paul's challenge should cause the Corinthian followers of Christ to grow up, as well. Although it's okay to start out immature, it's not okay to stay that way.

Paul hinted at the need for maturity before when he said, "We do, however, speak a message of wisdom among the mature" (1 Cor 2:6). We need this maturity to discern the voice of God's Spirit. In Corinth, instead of relying on the Spirit of God, the followers of Christ continued to rely on the wisdom of the world. They were looking for grown-up respectability, but Paul sees that they are only infants.

How does Paul know? What is the evidence that a follower of Christ has not grown up? Paul mentions three: "For since there is jealousy and quarreling among you, are you not worldly? Are you not acting like mere men? For when one says, 'I follow Paul,' and another, 'I follow Apollos,' are you not mere men?" (3:3b–4).

It's funny, isn't it? Jealousy, quarreling, and taking sides don't usually make my list of top ten sins. Yet for Paul, these are evidences of immaturity. This makes sense when we look at them in the context of valuing others. Jealousy doesn't see other people as gifts from God to the community. It is focused on self, on the promotion of one's own gifts, and on devaluing the gifts of others. As we saw in chapter 1, pointing out the faults of another member may increase our own status, as it did for Sally. Jealousy may come from forgetting that God has brought each of us into the assembly for the benefit of all.

Instead of working to make room for each person, the followers of Christ in Corinth were quarreling, which can also come from not valuing others. Even when quarreling has come from a real wrong someone has done, it needs to be addressed. We have to pull up the carpet and take care of the rocks that have gotten underneath it so that we don't keep tripping over them.

Ben Witherington, in *Making a Meal of It*, discusses the way the Lord's Supper is a "group-building ceremony." He interprets "the body of the Lord" as "the body of believers" (1 Cor 11:29).[5] Paul says that this body must be recognized. The sign of peace that some of our churches still practice fits into this understanding nicely. If I want to recognize the unity of the body, I may need to walk across the sanctuary and shake hands with someone with whom I have a strained relationship. I may need to set aside some time and follow the procedure laid out in Matt 18:15–20 so that the body can be whole again.

Taking sides, too, shows immaturity that keeps us from hearing God's Spirit in community. Sometimes we can get our identity so wrapped up in being a follower of one Christian teacher or another that we lose our identity as a follower of Christ in our local church. We look at a brother or a sister and think with disdain, "Oh, that's right. *You* listen to Joel Osteen." Small circles form, each valuing its own leader above the others, making the other groups into outgroups, failing to remember the common calling of all followers of Christ. This behavior might be appropriate social positioning in Roman or American culture. In Christ, however, it needs to change.

God's community should be a family, yet, like children, we need to grow up. Jealousy of someone else's gifts, blessings, or church position, not speaking to brothers and sisters in Christ, taking sides based on quarrels or leadership, these are evidences of immaturity. We have to grow up if we want to be able to discern God's Spirit among all those other voices. Paul has replaced immature behaviors with boasting about God, remembering the common call, and depending on the wisdom given to the community by God's Spirit. As we think about applying this today, maybe we could broaden the application across denominations.

Football analogies seem to work well, although I confess I know nothing about football. But I could imagine representatives from all the churches in our town getting together in a huddle. The coach says, "Okay, you Baptists, you go get 'em! Hook 'em and bring 'em in and then send them over to the Methodists for discipleship. You Methodists, you sort them out. Send people who need healing to the non-denominational church down the street. If you find some academics, send them to help out the Presbyterians with their campus ministry. If you find any evangelists, send 'em back to the Baptists. Ready? Okay, let's go!"

---

5. Witherington, *Meal,* 59.

Although that analogy depends heavily on stereotypes and many churches are good at several different kinds of ministries, it does show the way we might think of valuing people with very different missions. Paul, who like me knew very little about football, offers several other analogies. In the next chapter, we will look at his word pictures for the community of Christ in Corinth.

Questions:

    1. Are you jealous of someone in your community?

    2. Are you not speaking to someone in your community?

    3. Do you side with one certain leader when conflicts occur?

    4. How could we help each other to grow up in these areas?

8

Followers of Christ Belong to God

1 Corinthians 3:5–23

John holds many titles at our church. He is a painter, a decorator, a lawn mower, a landscaper, a Sunday morning coffee maker, a men's group leader, an elected delegate to Annual Conference, and a member of the Pastor's Cabinet.

He explains, "My heart is to serve, and there are so many different ways that we can serve. Whether it's behind the curtain, whether it's in front of the curtain, they're all important things, and they all combine with each other. The Lord has blessed me with many gifts. Some of them might seem simple, like mowing the lawn or landscaping, but God gave me those gifts for a reason, not only for my own home, or my own enjoyment. This is God's church, and if he's given me these talents I just truly feel that I need to be using them."

~from an interview with John Cosner

WHAT ARE THE MOST important jobs in the church? We know the answer—no job is more important than another. Do we act that way, though? I love that John, as a church leader, is still willing to make the coffee on Sunday mornings.

B. T. Roberts is remembered today as the father of Free Methodism in America. This man embodied the identity we have been talking about. He followed the wisdom of God even when he lost all respectability in his original denomination. William Kendall was a friend of his, no less faithful, no less wise in God's Spirit. They encouraged each other through difficult times. But those in charge shuffled Kendall off to an out-of-the-way church. He preached there for about a year. People's lives were changed. Then he caught a fever and died. His name is in some history books, but he is not especially well remembered. He never got to see the results of his faithfulness.[1]

So—am I willing to be a William Kendall? Of course most of us would be willing to be a B. T. Roberts if God asked us to. We would be willing to suffer for awhile if we would eventually see our work have a lasting impact in God's kingdom. But what if I die and nobody remembers what I did? Even today, what if nobody notices my faithfulness? Do I, like the Corinthians, want to look important, or at least to be attached to someone else who is? Paul corrects this desire by putting leadership in the proper perspective.

A FIELD BELONGING TO GOD: 1 CORINTHIANS 3:5–8

"What, after all, is Apollos? And what is Paul? Only servants, through whom you came to believe" (3:5a). When Paul calls himself and Apollos *servants*, he is not using a term of respect! Plutarch, writing in the first and second century, believed that working "with one's own hands on lowly tasks" shows "one's own indifference to higher things."[2] Although manual laborers such as servants were not respected by some of the elite, Paul uses these terms for the leaders of the community. In the twenty-first century, we might imagine Paul calling our church leaders *waiters, busboys,* or *clerks.* Paul wanted the Corinthians to rethink the way they valued their leaders.

We already know that leaders should be servants. In fact, for us the title "servant of the Lord" actually brings a certain amount of respect. Paul goes on, though, to point away from them to the one standing behind them: "The Lord has assigned to each his task. I planted the seed, Apollos watered it" (3:5b –6a). This means that the leaders can't be judged according to usual criteria. They can only be judged by God, since he is the one who appointed them to their tasks. Since Paul shows here that he values the work of Apollos, the two men were probably not in competition with each other. They were able to see their ministries as complementary

1. Marston, *Witness,* 189–91, 198–201.
2. Plutarch, *Pericles* 2.2.

and to identify themselves as servants of God living in Christ. But the Corinthians needed God's wisdom to evaluate their leaders correctly and to think of themselves as belonging to God rather than as members of a certain leader's circle.

Furthermore, although the servants planted the seed, "God made it grow. So neither he who plants nor he who waters is anything, but only God, who makes things grow" (3:6b–7). Both here and in verse 5 (where he mentions the time that the Corinthians "came to believe") Paul reminds the Corinthians of the planting of the community when they committed themselves to living life in Christ. He also turns their attention away from their leaders and towards God whose power was there at the beginning and continues to keep them growing. This connects the Corinthians with each other, but in an identity based on God rather than based on a human leader. After all, the purpose of farm work is to make things grow, and only God can provide the power for that.

This common purpose pulls everybody together into their common identity in Christ. "The man who plants and the man who waters have one purpose, and each will be rewarded according to his own labor" (3:8). God rewards, so again the Corinthians need to concentrate on his evaluation. The focus on God continues in the next verse: "For we are co-workers who belong to God; you are a field that belongs to God" (3:9a).[3] Paul emphasizes unity of purpose under God's ownership for the growth of the community. This is the correct attitude for mature followers of Christ.

Paul looks beyond the leaders to the one assigning their tasks, and he sees each task as a mission given by God. How can we evaluate our own leaders and communities according to God's wisdom? How can we keep our focus on God's power at work among us?

One analogy that helps me—because I am a mother and not a farmer—is comparing the church to my family. We are all God's children, and sometimes we act just like mine did at home. "He's not doing the dishes right!" Or more subtly, "Mom, she still hasn't done the dishes like you asked." But the faithfulness of one child is not the business of the other. Usually, the tattler has misunderstood the assignment. The one forgets how much I love the other.

---

3. Translation from Tucker, *You Belong*, 216–17.

If God has assigned a specific task to someone else, who am I to criticize? How would I know what God asked her to do? If his ministry isn't growing as fast as I think it should, how can I judge? Maybe God has appointed him to plant rather than to water. How dare I point out to God someone else's sins? He already knows and grieves over them.

These kinds of divisions and social positioning lead to the jealousy and quarrelling that Paul gave as evidence of immaturity. God has assigned jobs as he sees fit; God himself is in charge of the outcome, and he will judge his workers. We need to identify ourselves as part of the people that belong to God following leaders who are responsible to him. The field and its workers belong to God.

Questions:

1. What jobs are invisible or less valued in your church? Can you imagine your leaders doing those tasks?

2. When have you seen people put the health of the community ahead of their own thoughts on an issue? How could you do that in your own life?

3. Who do you see working in a ministry that is totally different from what you might be called to do?

4. How could you communicate to that person how valuable that ministry is to all of you?

A BUILDING BELONGING TO GOD—HIS TEMPLE: 1 CORINTHIANS 3:9–17

Paul continues to talk about a servant's responsibility to God as he moves into a different analogy. He refers again to the division of labor in God's work: "You are a building that belongs to God. According to the grace of God given to me, like a wise master-builder, I laid a foundation but another builds on it" (3:9b–10a).[4]

Paul's specific mission, of course, was the spread of the gospel to the gentiles—a missional mission. But even here he recognizes that there is nothing more honorable about that specific task. Although he was laying

---

4. Tucker, *You Belong*, 216–19.

a foundation, he was acting by God's grace, and someone else has to come to continue the work he started. In a construction project of this type, each job matters, and each person depends on Jesus Christ. "But each one should be careful how he builds. For no one can lay any foundation other than the one already laid, which is Jesus Christ" (3:10b–11).

Paul has now broadened his address beyond the leaders to everyone who has received grace from God. Accepting this gift, as we saw in chapter 4, establishes a relationship with responsibilities towards the giver. As the members of the community build themselves together, each has a task for which he is responsible to God. And since Jesus Christ is the foundation, a commitment to living together in Christ is a foundational requirement.

We saw that since God assigned each task, only he can decide how well each one is done. However, before we discuss God's future judgment, we have to look at the greater context of this passage and see that Paul does not forbid all human judgment. In the previous chapter, we saw that "the spiritual man makes judgments about all things" (2:15). In chapter 5 of this letter, Paul judges the behavior of a member of the assembly. In chapter 6, Paul tells his hearers that they should be able to judge disputes among themselves, although even there he ultimately suggests that they should be able to let go of their own need for justice. In 1 Corinthians 9, Paul gives a defense to those judging him. Also, several times he expects the Corinthians to be able to judge for themselves between right and wrong (1 Cor 10:15; 11:13). So human beings can evaluate each other, but as we saw in the last chapter, that evaluation has to be based on the wisdom that comes from God. However, in this section, Paul discusses the ultimate judgment that only God can make.

"If any man builds on this foundation using gold, silver, costly stones, wood, hay or straw, his work will be shown for what it is, because the Day will bring it to light. It will be revealed with fire, and the fire will test the quality of each man's work. If what he has built survives, he will receive his reward. If it is burned up, he will suffer loss; he himself will be saved, but only as one escaping through the flames" (3:12–15).

That's pretty sobering, isn't it? One way or another, for good or for bad, each person will have to answer to God. How will our work among God's people stand up to God's evaluation? After all, we won't be able to fool him. He will see each of our works for what it is. Just as a fire would burn up straw no matter how much it might be disguised as gold, and reveal gold no matter how dirty and scuffed it might have gotten, so God's gaze will reveal the reality of each person's work. William Kendall, for example, faithfully proclaimed the gospel of Christ in the small church where he was sent. Although to those who might evaluate his work on the basis of his reputation with the important people of his world what he accomplished might look like straw, God's evaluation of his obedience could easily reveal it to be gold. Paul encourages workers such as this in his day by reassuring them that they will receive a reward.

However, even if a worker's efforts do not survive, their own survival is not in jeopardy, unlike the Roman rulers they had been identifying with. So although this passage should not be seen as a threat, the knowledge of this coming evaluation should help the followers of Christ to recommit to the mission of Christ, building a community grounded in "faith, hope, and love" (1 Cor 13:13).

This mission incorporates both ladders that we looked at in chapter 2. Paul talked about his own role as an apostle, and we have seen that he is a model for the followers of Christ. He demonstrates what commitment to a specific role should look like. The Corinthians should obey God's call and find their roles in building their community.

At the same time Paul asks the Corinthians to put their commitment to their group identity first. They should be dedicated to living God's mission with each other. Their identity in Christ should be at the top of their ladder. Other commitments move down when they get in the way. Relationships with others don't need to be abandoned, though. Conversations and interactions with a variety of people and even memberships in other groups help the followers of Christ to define themselves and to figure out what it means for them to live in Christ.

Paul then adds one more element to this metaphor, one piece of information that changes everything. As the Corinthians looked around at their city with its many temples, they knew that each one held the statue of a god or goddess in an inner room. The priests of the temple would feed the statue, wash it, dress it, and perform the various rituals which that particular god required. The presence of a god turned the building into a temple.

Paul writes to this community of followers of Christ, calls them a building and then points to them and says, "Don't you know that you yourselves are God's temple and that God's Spirit lives in you?" (3:16). They are not just any building; they are a temple!

During the church service last Sunday, a baby started crying, and the parents waited a long time before taking him out. One of the speakers said something I disagreed with, and it frustrated me, and I wanted to correct her. The praise band started, but they were slow, and I couldn't sing without getting frustrated. Worship seemed impossible; everything felt off. Then I remembered: *This* is where God lives. In the midst of fussing babies, mistaken speakers, imperfect musicians, and impatient, critical me, God is here. The Holy Spirit chooses to live right in the middle of our community. His presence turns us into his temple.

His presence raises the requirements for the way we behave, too. After all, temple behavior is different from street behavior. The call of God, which Paul first introduced in 1 Cor 1:1–2, is a call to holiness. All of us, the followers of Christ together, are sacred, dedicated to God. That implies, not proper, respectable behavior, but holy behavior empowered by his Spirit.

This behavior is different from that which is expected in the Roman world. Social positioning that puts a person's status ahead of others tears down the community. Destroying an ordinary building might be okay, but "If anyone destroys God's temple, God will destroy him; for God's temple is sacred, and you are that temple" (3:17). This predicts a pretty severe response to anyone guilty of tearing it down. Speaking and acting in ways that harm the unity of followers of Christ are attacks against the holy temple of God.

Questions:

1. Are there people or ministries that you need to trust to God's judgment on the last day?

2. How does this picture of the last day help you to evaluate your commitment to living in Christ?

3. How does your mission, your specific role in the Christian community, rely on God and cooperate with others?

4. Can you envision your local community of followers of Christ as the place where the Holy Spirit lives? How can you help to make it holy?

A PEOPLE BELONGING TO GOD: 1 CORINTHIANS 3:18–23

The people of Corinth would have boasted about the leaders they were attached to. The status of a client depended on the status of his patron, so the slave of a magistrate had more respect than the slave of a merchant. You could take pride in your patron or your owner.

This sounds strange until we think of the ways we identify ourselves with those we follow, as well. When the politician we voted for is ridiculed in the media, we may feel ashamed or get defensive. When we talk with other people, we figure out who follows this or that athlete, this or that singer, this or that author, and judge them accordingly. We become attached to our local leaders, as well. Although these loyalties help us to grow, to model ourselves after those we follow, in Corinth these same loyalties had started to divide people.

So Paul uses the words of a fool to turn this thinking upside down. In literature, fools often say lines that hide the truth in playfulness. In *The Twelfth Night*, the fool pokes fun at Olivia's elaborate show of grief by pointing out that if she is mourning, she should have reason to mourn, but since her brother is in heaven, she has no reason to mourn, so she is actually a fool.[5] This kind of wit was used even in antiquity. Diogenes the Cynic who lived in the third century B.C. wanted to make people question the accepted behavior of his time. One day when he was sunning himself, Alexander the Great "came and stood over him and said, 'Ask of me any boon you like.' To which he replied, 'Stand out of my light.'"[6]

Paul also suggests playing the fool: "Do not deceive yourselves. If any one of you thinks he is wise by the standards of this age, he should become a 'fool' so that he may become wise. For the wisdom of this world is foolishness in God's sight. As it is written: 'He catches the wise in their craftiness'" (3:18–19). Paul quotes Job 5:13 to show that God doesn't necessarily support those who do what seems smart. In fact, these smart things will trip them up in the end.

He then quotes Psalm 94:11, "The Lord knows that the thoughts of the wise are futile" (3:20). In that psalm, the smart people, the ones who value the respect of the important people in their world, are also proud, wicked, arrogant, boastful oppressors. The psalm ends with the assurance that God "will repay them for their sins and destroy them for their wick-

5. Shakespeare, *Twelfth*, 1.5.58–62.
6. Diogenes, *Lives of Eminent Philosophers* 6.2.6.

edness" (Ps 94:23). Smart people take care of number one. Smart people keep their mouths shut when someone in power does something wrong. Smart people drop names. Smart people keep their own social status and advancement in mind. God knows their thoughts and will destroy them. The behavior that is smart for society does not ultimately work with God. "So then, no more boasting about men!" (3:21a).

Diogenes had said: "Everything belongs to the Gods; and the Gods are friends to the wise; and all the property of friends is held in common; therefore everything belongs to the wise."[7] If this is so, then wise people—and who doesn't claim to be wise?—can do anything they want. Paul picks up where Diogenes left off, "All things are yours, whether Paul or Apollos or Cephas or the world or life or death or the present or the future—all are yours" (3:21b–22). But he draws a completely different conclusion, "and you belong to Christ, and Christ belongs to God" (3:23).[8] Every kind of behavior is not acceptable as Diogenes said. Paul overturns this conclusion by overturning previous ideas of leadership. Rather than followers of Christ belonging to the leaders, the leaders belong to the people. In fact, everything belongs to the people . . . but then, they belong to Christ and ultimately to God.

This discussion of belonging connects with our group identity. When we choose to belong to a group, the leaders become our models. We attach ourselves to them. We work for their glory because that glory becomes ours. Then we can brag about the leaders that we follow. Smart people do this, in the twenty-first century as well as in the first.

But Paul says, don't be smart. Be a fool. Your leader is your servant. Evaluate all your activities in light of Christ's return. All sorts of people—men and women, Jewish and Greek, slave and free—have been baptized into the body of Christ, but these identities, although still present, should no longer have the strongest influence on behavior. Remember, your behavior should reflect the fact that you belong to Christ, and Christ belongs to God.

Questions:

1. When have you gone against "what everyone expected" to follow the wisdom of God?

7. Diogenes, *Lives of Eminent Philosophers* 6.2.6.
8. Tucker, *You Belong,* 233.

2. How does it change how you think about your leaders if they belong to you rather than you belonging to them? If you are a leader, how does it change how you think about yourself?

3. "All things belong to you." Later in the letter, twice in fact, Paul says, "'Everything is permissible'—but not everything is beneficial" (1 Cor 6:12; 10:23). What can you do to further the health and holiness of your community? What are you tempted to do that is ultimately destructive?

4. How does Paul's final reminder, "you belong to Christ and Christ belongs to God," strengthen the identity of the Christian community?

9

Followers of Christ Belong Together

1 Corinthians 4:1–21

On Tuesday, January 12, 2010, a 7.0 earthquake struck near Port-au-Prince, Haiti. An early video showed the ruins of a school with people of all ages sitting on blankets under tarps. A Haitian man provided the opening comments, "Suddenly, everybody . . . everywhere . . . people start to die. It is very, very difficult." Words rolled up on the screen: "This is our Family, Our Free Methodist family in Haiti, Suffering."

~from the video Help Haiti Heal[1]

ON THE SUNDAY AFTER the earthquake, we sat in church watching this video. At first, I was watching the people of Haiti suffer. I felt badly for them. But when those words rolled up on the screen, my throat tightened and my eyes teared up. I was suddenly watching my family suffer. The word *family* turned *them* into *us*. In 1 Corinthians 4, Paul continues to build the followers of Christ into a family, and he teaches them that suffering should be an expected part of their identity.

JUDGING IN THE COMMUNITY: 1 CORINTHIANS 4:1–5

Before using the language of family again, though, Paul repeats some of his previous comments, reversing the status of leaders. "Let each person

1. http://reelfm.tv/2010/01/haiti-church/ (Help Haiti Heal, 2010, Free Methodist World Missions, Indianapolis, IN).

think about us in this manner, as servants of Christ and as stewards of God's mysteries" (4:1).[2] As the community evaluates Paul and the other leaders, they should see them as simply servants. Paul also uses the word *steward*, usually a slave who ran the household for the owner. Although he had the master's trust, he did not own any of the goods himself. Paul asks those who follow Christ to think of their leaders in this way, as stewards of the plan that God had kept secret before but is now revealing.

"Now it is required that those who have been given a trust must prove faithful" (4:2). The main requirement of servants and stewards is faithfulness. Paul will bring this up again in verse 17 when he discusses Timothy's qualifications. Faithfulness also described God, so it should be an important value in the community's identity in Christ (1 Cor 1:9). God has given grace and that requires faithfulness on our part.

As God's people act according to his wisdom, their actions will continue to confuse others. In 1 Cor 2:14–15, Paul already established that people without God's Spirit don't have the ability to evaluate correctly. Now he extends the ban on judgment even further. "I care very little if I am judged by you or by any human court; indeed, I do not even judge myself. My conscience is clear, but that does not make me innocent. It is the Lord who judges me" (4:3–4). We saw in the last chapter that no one has the ability to judge, not the community, not the surrounding culture. Here Paul adds himself to the list. If the Corinthians' previous judgments were based on the standards of the Roman world, then it makes sense for Paul to question their ability to judge correctly. Even with God's Spirit, Paul, as a model for the community, does not have the resources to judge himself. That means that we don't have the ability to judge ourselves correctly either. No one on earth has the resources for that.

"Therefore judge nothing before the appointed time; wait till the Lord comes. He will bring to light what is hidden in darkness and will expose the motives of men's hearts" (4:5a). As in 1 Cor 3:13, the timing has been pushed back. Once motives are revealed, "At that time each will receive his praise from God" (4:5b). Paul is confident that God will praise the followers of Christ in Corinth. This would have encouraged them. They could continue to listen for God's Spirit to guide their community and to direct them in their individual roles. If God is the one to judge, he is also the one to follow.

2. Tucker, *You Belong*, 236.

This reminder to recognize the hidden nature of motives helps us today, too. Without persecution, it is easy for us to evaluate ourselves and others based on the assumptions of our culture. When a young man last week came up to me and told me about his career, I thought he was bragging. On the other hand, when something good happens to me, I want to tell people, too. As best as I can tell, it's because I want them to rejoice with me; I don't think it is pride . . . but how would I know? It's quite possible that the young man I spoke to was just looking for others to share his joy. It's quite possible that I have pride that's so well hidden that I can't see it myself. It's easy to assume good motives for ourselves and our friends, and bad motives for everyone else.

The assumptions of our culture can get so attached to us that we don't even notice them. We wear them like blinders; they limit our sight, and we are shocked when we suddenly smack our heads up against another point of view. Judgments are best left to God, who can see clearly.

Let's remember in our judgments, then, that we don't see motives. Let's ask for the help of God's Spirit for the evaluations that do need to be made. Let's focus on straightening out our own motives as best we can. And let's look forward to the revelation, when we will receive God's praise.

Questions:

1. Have you ever mistakenly judged someone because you didn't understand their motives?

2. On what basis are you evaluated in non-Christian circles?

3. How can we recognize that only God can judge correctly, but still make the judgments necessary to choose friends and people for various positions in the church?

4. What are your motives for the roles you play?

SUFFERING IN THE COMMUNITY: 1 CORINTHIANS 4:6–13

As a leader, Paul continues to model a balance between authority and empowerment. He keeps reminding the followers of Christ that he is one of them: "Now, brothers" (4:6a). At the same time, he does not hesitate to give them advice. God has appointed him as one of their leaders, and yet leaders are called to serve.

In Paul's previous instructions, he used well-known leaders as examples. "I have figuratively applied my teaching to myself and Apollos because of you, so that in us you may learn not to go beyond what is written" (4:6a).[3] By using examples, he didn't embarrass the Corinthian leaders. But what is this written thing that they are not supposed to go beyond?

Normally, when Paul talks about what is written he then writes a quotation: "As it is written: 'Let him who boasts boast in the Lord'" (1 Cor 1:31; Jer 9:24). But he doesn't do that here. Some scholars believe that Paul is referring to his own instructions to the Corinthians.[4] This would explain why he doesn't give a specific quotation. Paul's writing had authority in the community, and he does not want them to go beyond his guidance.

After all, Paul wanted them to boast in the Lord, but instead they were boasting in their leaders. He has been addressing this problem since 1 Cor 1:10, and here he brings it up again: "Then you will not take pride in one man over against another" (4:6b). Going beyond boasting in God to boasting in leaders was causing some of the friction in the community. We will see in the next few verses that they had gone beyond Paul's instructions in other ways, as well.

Next Paul asks, "For who makes you different from anyone else?" (4:7a). There *were* differences among the Corinthians. They had different genders, different ethnicities, differences of status. In 1 Cor 7:20, he urges each one "to remain in the situation which he was in when God called him." That verse always makes me think of a phrase I used to see all the time: Bloom where you are planted. Each of our situations gives us a new way to live the values of an identity based in Christ.

Since Paul expects some of these differences to remain, he does not ask, "*What* makes you different?" The problem was not the differences but the way the Corinthians were evaluating those differences, the way they were giving more or less honor to each one. The important question

---

3. Tucker, *You Belong*, 240.

4. Ibid., 241–42. In 1 Cor 14:37, for example, Paul wants anyone who "thinks he is a prophet or spiritually gifted" to "acknowledge that what I am writing to you is the Lord's command." This shows that he recognizes at least some of his own writing to be God's command.

should not have been who has the most status, but where did the differences come from?

The implied answer, of course, is God. If the Corinthians recognize that their differences were given to them by God, they can stop using them to rank each other. "What do you have that you did not receive? And if you did receive it, why do you boast as though you did not?" (4:7b). Since they have received all they have, they are *all* clients; none of them are patrons. The whole community is dependent on the giver, God. This makes all boasting inappropriate, whether in your leader or in the number of your followers. Only boasting in God makes any sense (1 Cor 1:27–31).

Paul continues with four exclamations which describe the way Paul saw the followers of Christ identifying themselves: "Already you have all you want! Already you have become rich! You have become kings—and that without us! How I wish that you really had become kings so that we might be kings with you!" (4:8). Here is another way in which the Corinthians had gone beyond what Paul had written. Beyond Paul, beyond God, they had set themselves up according to their society with everything they needed. They felt like kings! Paul is going to contrast this identity with the identity of the apostles, an identity of suffering, one that the community needs to adopt instead.

In addition to going beyond Paul's instructions, these exclamations speak of possessions, riches, and rulers. These relate to honor and power, the very areas that were causing problems for the Corinthians. So Paul uses two word pictures to correct their misunderstanding. In the first, he shows that suffering is an inevitable result of living in Christ. Although leadership in other contexts might imply honor, among followers of Christ it brings suffering. The lack of conflict which the Corinthians had experienced allowed them to miss this connection. Paul reminds them of his own suffering, of the other apostles' suffering, and ultimately of Jesus' suffering, as well (2 Cor 1:5). To do this, he uses a word picture.

"For it seems to me that God has put us apostles on display at the end of the procession, like men condemned to die in the arena" (4:9a). Roman games in the arena displayed courage and virtue, reinforced the power of Rome, and brought various conquered nations together in a common pastime. At these games, gladiators fought and died in staged battles, and criminals were executed. Seneca, in the first century A.D., describes the treatment of the condemned: "All the trifling is put aside and it is pure murder. The men have no defensive armor. They are exposed to blows at all points, and no one ever strikes in vain . . . the outcome of every fight is death."[5]

Paul is just one leader among the rest, and their position at the end of the procession shows the difference between the order of things in Rome and in Christ. Those whom the Corinthians are putting at the top of the social scale are instead, in Paul's analogy, at the bottom. Suffering in Christ works differently than suffering in the Roman world does. Rather than being a marker of shame, it is a valued part of an identity based in Christ.[6]

Of course, the image of the condemned criminal is also a reminder of Jesus' crucifixion. Jesus suffered publically, and Paul continues to describe suffering as a part of identity in Christ (Mark 8:31; 9:31; 10:33–34; Phil 1:29–30). "We have been made a spectacle to the whole universe, to angels as well as to men" (4:9b). God has allowed the apostles to be disgraced in the eyes of the world, but more than just the world is watching. One cannot follow Christ and still expect or desire honor from the world. The identity of Christ and the identity of the first leaders included suffering. It should therefore be a part of the Corinthians' identity in Christ.

Paul's next words connect with 1 Cor 1:18–21 where he established the difference between the world's ideas of wisdom and God's. "We are fools for Christ, but you are so wise in Christ!" (4:10a). God's wisdom, which looks so foolish, comes from God's Spirit. So the apostles have embraced foolishness as they embraced Christ. Old Testament prophets often obeyed God to the point of foolishness, too.[7] This contrasts with the Corinthians' idea of living in Christ, which seems to have included some idea of shrewdness.[8] They saw their membership in the community as something that would help them live well.

The next exclamation would come as a shock to those who regularly competed for power. "We are weak, but you are strong!" (4:10b). Why would the Corinthians want to follow someone weak? Of *course*, they wanted strong leaders. But leaders in this community of Christ should not look for power as a badge of honor. The Corinthians had gone beyond what Paul had told them.

5. Seneca, *Epistles* 7.3–5.

6. See, however, some limits to this in chapter 10.

7. Ezekiel, for example, mounted a siege against a drawing of Jerusalem (Ezek 4).

8. The Greek here is not the same word for *wise* that Paul has used up to now, but means sensible or possibly shrewd.

Finally, Paul brings them back to concepts of honor and shame. "You are honored, we are dishonored!" (4:10c). Dishonor meant, for example, leaving unburied the corpses of those condemned to death. The Corinthians' expectation of the honor they would receive as a part of their identity in Christ is completely reversed. Although tempted to see themselves as somehow above suffering, possibly even as a result of their own wise efforts, Paul calls them to a new vision of the gospel. In all of these ways, in their ideas of wisdom, power, and honor, the Corinthians have gone beyond what Paul intended for them.

Next, Paul models the suffering in his own life and in the lives of the other apostles. "To this very hour we go hungry and thirsty, we are in rags, we are brutally treated, we are homeless" (4:11). The values of this identity come not only from the leaders of the movement, but also from Jesus. He, too, described for his disciples an identity that included suffering. His parables spoke about it: "For I was hungry and you gave me something to eat, I was thirsty and you gave me something to drink, I was a stranger and you invited me in, I needed clothes and you clothed me, I was sick and you looked after me, I was in prison and you came to visit me" (Matthew 25:35–36). He taught it: "Then a teacher of the law came to him and said, 'Teacher, I will follow you wherever you go.' Jesus replied, 'Foxes have holes and birds of the air have nests, but the Son of Man has no place to lay his head'" (Matthew 8:19–20). He modeled it in his own life: "Then they spit in his face and struck him with their fists. Others slapped him" (Matthew 26:67–68).

Paul then adds dishonor to his description of an identity based in Christ: "We work hard with our own hands" (4:12a). Manual labor was beneath the elites of the Roman Empire, and a sore point between the Corinthians and Paul since he chose to work rather than to accept gifts from them (1 Cor 9:6, 12–23). So hard work is another element in the identity of Christ followers that would earn them the disrespect of the world.

And yet, while disrespected, a follower of Christ offers respect: "When we are cursed, we bless; when we are persecuted, we endure it; when we are slandered, we answer kindly" (4:12b–13a). Responding to cursing with blessing does not seem wise. Persecution implies a lack of power. Slander communicates dishonor. But the responses of a person whose identity is based in Christ come from Jesus' teaching: "Bless those who curse you, pray for those who mistreat you" (Luke 6:28). He also acted this way himself: "Jesus said, 'Father, forgive them, for they do not know what they are doing'" (Luke 23:34). And those who remembered him described him in this way: "When they hurled their insults at him, he did not retaliate; when he suffered, he made no threats. Instead, he entrusted himself to him who judges justly" (1 Pet 2:23). If those who follow Christ identify with him, they will behave this way, too. The Corinthians, however, had gone not only beyond Paul, but even beyond Jesus. They had gone beyond the identity based in Christ that Paul was trying to form in them through his teaching and his writing.

Paul ends this picture with a final image of suffering. "Up to this moment we have become the scum of the earth, the refuse of the world" (4:13b). These, of course, are not honorable terms, but they come with the calling of God, along with his mission and his Spirit (1 Cor 1:2). The Corinthian followers of Christ had to include suffering and dishonor among the values of their own identity, rather than seeing it as something that only happened to others.

Churches in the United States, also not very persecuted, may need these reminders, too. As members of the religion which has most influenced our culture, we have had the luxury of dividing ourselves based on our preferred leaders, and we pride ourselves on our distinctive identities. With regard to the rest of the world, Americans are those-who-have-and-can-give. This giving can involve self-denial, but sometimes pride, too. We are rarely those-who-suffer.

As members of the Not-Very-Persecuted Church, we can get uncomfortable with that comfort and prosperity. We sense that we, too, have gone beyond the identity of suffering given to us in the Bible. We have to embrace a different picture of suffering, one that includes looking weak and foolish in our world.

Questions:

1. What are you tempted to brag about besides God?

2. What missions has God called you to?

3. How have you risked looking foolish, weak, or disrespected in those missions?

4. How is God calling you to a mission where you risk looking foolish, weak, or disrespected today?

MODELS FOR THE COMMUNITY: 1 CORINTHIANS 4:14–17

Moms are well known for their ability to inflict guilt. All we have to do is talk about hours of labor or sleepless nights, and violins start playing in the background. When we bring up our suffering or correct our children in public, we can embarrass them. Paul was correcting the Corinthians' identity in Christ, but he wants to make sure that they don't misunderstand his motives: "I am not writing this to shame you, but as my beloved children—to teach you" (4:14).[9] Paul distances himself from any kind of power play. Shame is not his purpose.

The word Paul uses here for *teach* is also used in Romans 15:14, where followers of Christ are told that they are "competent to *instruct* one another." This word fits well with the rest of 1 Corinthians 4, which echoes with references to education. Paul talks about instruction, guardians, imitation, reminding, teaching, and a stick. This is Paul's second word picture as he reshapes the Corinthians' identity in Christ.

Education in the Roman world was usually reserved for boys. A guardian walked the son to school and taught him proper Roman behavior. Children became close to their guardians, but Paul contrasts this relationship with the boy's love for his father. "Even though you have ten thousand guardians in Christ, you do not have many fathers, for in Christ Jesus I became your father through the gospel" (4:15). The Corinthian followers of Christ would of course have ties to those who taught them, but Paul urges them to pay attention to his words since, by telling the good news of Christ, he fathered them. You obey your guardian, but your father is the one you want to imitate.

"Therefore," Paul says, "I urge you to imitate me" (4:16). A father would become a role model for a young Roman boy, but he would have other models, too. Quintilian in the first century A.D. gives these instructions for educating orators:

> One will never regret making sure that, when the child (according to the usual practice) begins to write names, he does not waste his time on common words that occur all the time. . . . I should like to suggest that the lines set for copying should not be meaningless sentences, but should convey some moral lesson. The memory of

9. Tucker, *You Belong,* 259.

such things stays with us till we are old, and the impression thus
made on the unformed mind will be good for the character also.[10]

A Roman boy would imitate his father, copy his lessons, and learn
to shape his own character in imitation of words written by the models
for Roman society. What should the Corinthians imitate? The new evaluation of suffering which Paul has just told them about. But why are they
imitating him? Because he is imitating Christ (1 Cor 11:1).

Paul is not asking them to imitate him only in suffering, but also in
his whole "way of life" (4:17). This, however, could have created a problem
for the Corinthians. As a Jewish follower of Christ, the values that Paul
had absorbed as a Pharisee took on new priorities but remained a part
of who Paul was. He could not be a perfect model for the Corinthians
because they had to reprioritize Roman values, not Jewish ones. Paul
could give them instruction in this process, but Timothy would be able
to model it for them. "For this reason I am sending to you Timothy, my
son whom I love, who is faithful in the Lord. He will remind you of my
way of life in Christ Jesus, which agrees with what I teach everywhere in
every church" (4:17).

Timothy was thoroughly grounded in Judaism through the teaching
of his mother and grandmother, and yet he must have grown up within
the cultural expectations of Rome since his Greek father did not allow
him to be circumcised as a baby (Acts 16:1–3; 2 Tim 1:5). Paul introduces
him to the Corinthians as a member of the family. He will be able to show
them how to live out an identity based in Christ in the Roman world.
Paul could continue to teach the Corinthians through Timothy, and they
both would keep them connected with the rest of the followers of Christ
around their world.

As we evaluate models for our Christian communities, we need the
balance that Paul gives us. We have to look for people who have taken
the identity of our culture and shifted it in Christ, so that we can still
maintain our outside relationships but keep the values of living in Christ
at the top of our ladder. These will be the people we can imitate, people
who fit our specific context, like Timothy, but understand the way people
live in Christ worldwide, like Paul.

---

10. Quintilian, *The Orator's Education* 1.1.34–36. A similar function for memory and
character development is found in Williams, "Abraham," 209–12.

Questions:

1. Who have been your guardians in Christ? Who was your father or mother?

2. Who do you know who models a willingness to look foolish, weak, or disrespected?

3. How would a Christian from a different culture act differently than an American Christian?

4. Who do you know who puts you in touch with what God's people are doing worldwide?

POWER IN THE COMMUNITY: 1 CORINTHIANS 4:18–21

The word picture of the school worked well for Paul as he described the need for a good model for the followers of Christ, but this image had one element that Paul did not want. The Roman educational system depended on power to enforce obedience, and Paul corrects that for the Corinthians.

For one thing, although Paul points out the people's arrogance, he does not name anyone specifically. "Some of you have become arrogant, as if I were not coming to you" (4:18). If he had said, for example, "Lucas, Martius, and even Crispus have become arrogant," this would have shamed those he named, especially since the letter would be read aloud to everyone. Instead, Paul lets the Corinthians figure out for themselves who he is referring to. He doesn't single anyone out, but he lets the followers of Christ know that arrogance is not part of an identity in Christ. Why were people behaving arrogantly?

Education may have been overemphasized, since Paul refers to the arrogant in the context of learning and teaching (4:6, 18–19). Roman values of power and wisdom may have been sources of pride, as Paul mentioned earlier. In 5:2, the Corinthians' pride relates to a man sleeping with his father's wife, so their understanding of masculinity may have needed correction. In 8:1, Paul addresses pride within the Corinthians' continuing involvement in the worship of idols and this, once again, reveals that they had not yet adjusted their behavior according to the cross. Paul goes on in 8:1 and in 13:4 to change the standards of their community by pointing out that "knowledge puffs up, but love builds up" and love "is not proud." In all of these ways, then, the Corinthians had not yet adjusted their thinking in Christ.

All along, Paul has been giving the Corinthians new descriptions of the followers of Christ, the group to which they now belong. In 1 Cor 1:21, they were "those who believe." In 2:12, they were "those who have received the Spirit who is from God." In 4:9, they belonged with the apostles "on display at the end of the procession, like men condemned to die in the arena," so suffering was to be expected among them. In 4:13, they answered kindly when slandered, and "have become the scum of the earth, the refuse of the world." Paul calls the Corinthians to a new understanding of who they are, without the arrogance of the value system of the Roman Empire.

Paul plans a visit, and at that time he would be able to tell how much the Corinthians had conformed to an identity based in Christ. "But I will come to you very soon, if the Lord is willing, and then I will find out not only how these arrogant people are talking, but what power they have" (4:19). Others may rely on arrogant talk but the Corinthians should value power. It is not the same as power in a Roman educational setting, power over people. Instead, it is the kind of power Paul has been talking about since the beginning of the letter, the power of the message of the cross, of Christ, and of the Spirit (1 Cor 1:18, 24, 2:4–5).[11] This is the same kind of power that Paul himself has been modeling.

"For the kingdom of God is not a matter of talk but of power" (4:20). Paul does not use the term "kingdom of God" very often, maybe because of the fundamental differences between an identity in Christ and the value system one would expect in a kingdom. Here, though, Paul spells out the differences: the Roman Empire might value arrogance and physical force, but the kingdom of God values the power of love and a humble spirit (4:21).

"What do you wish; shall I come to you with a stick, or with love in a spirit of humility?" (4:21).[12] This verse offers the Corinthian followers of Christ a choice between the two group identities. If they truly prefer to

11. A more detailed and scholarly discussion of issues of power can be found in Ehrensperger, *Dynamics*.

12. Tucker, *You Belong*, 266–67. The stick of training was often a part of the educational process and connects with Proverbs 22:15, "Folly is bound up in the heart of a child, but the rod of discipline will drive it far from him." This stick would then be a part of the expected methods of teaching, discipline, and correction for the young.

align themselves with the dominant culture of their day, if they are going to act like immature children fighting with each other and competing for power and honor, then according to their own logic, Paul as their father would need to correct them with a stick.

This, however, is not what Paul would prefer. He does not advocate the use of boasting to compete for honor, or power to control others. Instead, he invites the Corinthians to adopt an identity that includes suffering and humility. In that case, Paul could continue to respond to them with gentleness.

How would we answer this same question? Honestly, if Paul came to visit my church, would I be one of the arrogant ones? Is the ministry I am involved in structured according to motivations of power borrowed from our culture? Or do we see evidence of the power of the cross, the mind of Christ, and an identity in Christ of humility and love?

Paul will continue to address the Corinthians on many of these topics in the rest of the letter, but we will stop here in order sift this analysis of Paul's words and apply his teaching to our lives.

Questions:

1. Do you use power to control or to empower others?

2. Does your community respect people who lead with humility?

3. How do you feel when a leader shows weakness?

4. How are the power of God and the wisdom of Christ displayed in your community?

10

The Not-Very-Persecuted Church Today

Carole works with university students from all over the world. Her mission is "creating a community that draws students into relationship with one another and with Jesus."

In a multicultural setting, feeling foolish can happen easily. Carole says that it's important to talk about the differences, to ask questions publicly so everyone understands. But even so one is bound to make mistakes.

One morning very early, Carole was driving a Chinese student to take an exam that would decide if she would be accepted at MIT. "There was this spider crawling on my steering wheel and I sort of brushed it away, tried to hit it. And then it's on the glass, on the windshield inside the car and we're at a stoplight. And I just lean over and smack the spider. And she turns to me and says, 'Carole, why do you kill the lucky spider? I'm on my way to my GRE. And you kill the lucky spider.' And, I didn't know spiders were lucky for Chinese."

Then Matthew 18 becomes key. "When you have something against a brother, go to them directly." That isn't necessarily comfortable in anyone's culture. "And I think, too, just the ability to laugh at yourself and to know that you're going to make mistakes, you're going to kill that spider on the windshield. And then to ask for forgiveness quickly."

~from an interview with Carole Metzger

VALY TELLS THE GOSPEL in Romania even though many people no longer want to hear. A woman years ago yelled the gospel into stores. Nadia runs the risk of being misjudged by both Christians and Muslims as she lives her identity in Christ. John doesn't let honor in the church go to his head. And Carole feels foolish many times as she learns about the cultures of the people in the community she is building. They have given up a measure of social respect for the sake of their missions. They have chosen to step away from their cultural identity to live their identity in Christ.

TANGLED UP IN CULTURE

Paul told the Corinthians three times in chapter 7 of his letter that they should remain in the situation in which God called them. Married or unmarried, slave or free, circumcised or uncircumcised, "each one should retain the place in life that the Lord assigned to him and to which God has called him." Paul says, "This is the rule I lay down in all the churches" (1 Cor 7:17). This means staying in our particular corner of the world and figuring out how to live in Christ right there.[1]

This caused problems for the Corinthian followers of Christ, though. Since they were not persecuted, they could continue to be involved in the Roman world. They could take the gospel out, and others could come in and find Christ. But their boundaries became blurred, and their behavior did not change enough. They needed to be Roman Christians, but they were often just Roman Romans.

Other early Christians sometimes changed their identity too much. At first, some gentiles thought that to become followers of Christ, they needed to adopt Jewish cultural forms. Sometimes Jewish followers of Christ promoted this idea, because their own identity was so intertwined with their faith in Christ. In a similar way, American missionaries have sometimes taught a gospel mixed with Western culture to Asian and African people groups. In a totally different context, a twentieth-century missionary tells about people in New Guinea who, after accepting the gospel themselves, started sending out their own missionaries. The first tribe, the Danis, wore very little clothing, but the tribe they were working with, the Ogotuts, wore none. So the Danis gathered up donations of gourds and string skirts: "Now that they are becoming God's children, they should be clothed decently."[2] This example makes me chuckle, most-

---

1. This doesn't mean that God won't sometimes call us elsewhere, as Paul's life demonstrates.

2. Dekker and Neely, *Torches,* 137–38.

ly because I see how similar we are. When someone from one culture brings the good news of Jesus Christ to another, we can all have trouble separating what is Christian from what is culture.

When we identify this strongly with our own cultural values, we can fail to notice when they get in the way of God's mission. We are supposed to act like American Christians, but sometimes we just act like American Americans. We let Christ's mission become secondary.

We shouldn't abandon our culture completely, though. Its ideas about wisdom and power, like getting an education, a good job, saving money, and rising in position, can become tools in working for God's kingdom. In his writing, Paul used the athletic contests of his day in his analogies (1 Cor 9:24–27; 2 Tim 2:5). He talked about ordinary household structures and clothing (1 Corinthians 11). He sometimes worked at a trade to support himself (Acts 18:3). He very practically asked the Corinthians to set money aside every week for the collection for the poor (1 Cor 16:2). We, too, can feel free to participate in the activities and use the wisdom that our culture makes available to us. Even Jesus said, "Suppose one of you wants to build a tower. Will he not first sit down and estimate the cost to see if he has enough money to complete it?" (Luke 14:28). Maybe today he would have said, "Look before you leap."

Living in balance means evaluating the wisdom and power of our world in light of God's call. We don't have to reject all of it. We do need to reject any of it that gets in the way of our mission. We have to constantly be willing to look silly, to seem weak, and to be looked down on when we live our identity in Christ.

Questions:

1. How does Christianity in other cultures look different than American Christianity?

2. In what ways do you seem just like other Americans?

3. In what ways are you different because of your faith in Christ?

4. Are there places where God is calling you to look more foolish and weak for the sake of loyalty to Christ?

FOOLISHNESS AND SUFFERING IN CHRIST

It's not necessary to take Paul's words to extremes to follow his example, though. Sometimes, we seem to use foolishness as another form of competition. "I'm a better Christian than you are because I do crazier things for Jesus!" Instead, some of the ways we are like the world around us can serve as bridges for communication. We need to balance our knowledge of our culture with a willingness to lose respect in that culture for the sake of living in Christ. If we begin to trust in the effectiveness of marketing, if we compete for the admiration of the community, if we worry about being laughed at more than we want to follow the Spirit of God, we may have forgotten our beginnings, lost sight of the cross of Christ and its foolishness, and stopped relying on the power and wisdom of God. Our identity in Christ must stay at the top of our ladder.

Living this identity may require that we suffer. Suffering in the Not-Very-Persecuted Church looks a little different than suffering in other times and places. Those Christians lost eyes, limbs, and lives. We have to give up our own preferences, we may be misunderstood and rejected, we may be passed over for promotion even in the church. Whatever waits for us tomorrow, let's be sure that we take advantage of opportunities for God's mission today.

Because we have read the Bible, we know the value of suffering. We recognize that suffering *should* be part of our identity in Christ. Since we don't regularly experience it, though, we may mistakenly try to include it in our identity in two different ways.

Because we know that living in Christ can produce suffering, we may get mixed up and think that suffering is always a result of living in Christ. I did something similar when I was a little girl. My mother used to give me daily spoonfuls of cod liver oil because of the vitamins in it. I don't know if you've ever tasted it, but cod liver oil is the nastiest, slimiest, worst-tasting liquid I have ever put in my mouth. Even once you swallow it, the taste stays with you all day long. But, it's good for you. Since cod liver oil and other healthy things like vaccinations are painful or at least uncomfortable, I decided that things that were painful must also be good for me. So whenever I had a scab or a bruise, I would poke and pinch it, thinking that would make it heal faster.

It seems to me that as Christians we sometimes do the same thing with suffering. Anything uncomfortable in our lives becomes evidence of our faithfulness to God. And when other people suffer, we may offer them our blessing and our prayers when we really should give them some help (Jas 2:16). Abuse and injustice continue because we know that Christians are supposed to suffer. Hopefully we don't cause suffering, but we can fail to fight against it.

An event in the gospel of Luke adds an important perspective to suffering in the identity of a Christian. It happened the day that Jesus read from the scroll of Isaiah in Nazareth. After he finished speaking to the people, they wanted to stone him. But Jesus "walked right through the crowd and went away" (Luke 4).

Jesus' death on the cross shows his willingness to suffer for the mission God had given him. But in this passage we see that he was not willing to suffer just any day, for any reason. He let them crucify him, but he did not let them throw him off a cliff. What was the difference? The difference was mission. The cross, he knew (as we see in the garden of Gethsemane), was his mission. This, however—being thrown off a cliff in Nazareth—was not. This day was the reverse of that day on the cross. We are called to suffer in obedience to God's call to a specific mission. We are allowed to walk away when no mission is involved. Only the mind of Christ, given to the community of followers of Christ and discerned through maturity, can tell us the difference. Suffering is part of our identity, but only suffering in pursuit of the call of God.

The picture of the apostles suffering in the arena that we discussed in chapter 9 can mistakenly cause us to react in a different way, as well. We know that Christians in the past have suffered and died for their faith. We hear about martyrs in other parts of the world today, and we believe that we will probably be next. So we imagine ourselves in that arena, standing in an alcove waiting for our turn. In the meantime, we think that our job is to strengthen ourselves in the faith and to prepare for suffering.

Although we may someday have to suffer physical persecution, standing on the side and waiting does not seem like the best response for us today. Instead, we should be at work in the arena itself, recognizing that persecution in the Not-Very-Persecuted Church looks more like dishonor and powerlessness than physical pain. As we find our role in the mission of Christ through his Spirit, we may look foolish and weak.

Almost 20 years ago, my friend Dan felt called to a new ministry. At that time, all of the men in his church wore suits on Sundays. Dan didn't like wearing suits. Besides, he knew that many other men felt the same way. He wanted men to be able to come to his church and feel welcome, even if they didn't own a suit. So he started "The Ministry of the Sweater." Every Sunday morning, he wore a sweater to church. Eventually, other men also began to show up in sweaters. In the end, his church did become a place where suits were not an unspoken requirement. But to get there, someone had to run the risk of looking foolish and feeling out of place. Dan saw an opportunity and answered God's call to a specific mission that fit him.

Questions:

1. When has living in Christ led you to feel foolish?

2. When has living in Christ led you to look weak?

3. Have you ever done something foolish or looked weak and realized later that it wasn't for the sake of God's mission but rather to draw attention to yourself or to compete with other Christians?

4. Are you risking your reputation in the choices you are making for Christ today?

IDENTITY IN MISSION FOR CHRIST

The first four chapters of 1 Corinthians teach us to recognize that not being persecuted gives us opportunities to live out our identity in Christ. We have to resist becoming alienated from others but also resist adopting their values, and instead take advantage of our specific culture. God calls and gives grace and gifts for the purpose of mission. The way we do or don't participate in the rest of culture depends on the calling and empowerment of God's Spirit. We have the mind of Christ. As we listen for God's call to mission for ourselves, let us also be kind to each other. Our missions may look different. We may make different choices about which parts of our culture to follow and which to reject based on the wisdom that God's Spirit gives. We need to listen to the ways that we might hear that Spirit through each other, and evaluate carefully what each person says and does as we decide whom to follow. Final judgments, however, we should leave up to God.

What are the missions God is calling you to? I don't know! The Holy Spirit is creative, and a building needs a lot of work. Maybe your role is foundational—that of providing a groundwork of prayer. Maybe your role is relational—connecting people to people in a bridgework of one-on-one conversations. Maybe your role is in construction itself—putting people together and motivating them to accomplish other missions for God. Maybe you are mortar—joining lots of others in a task too big for anyone to accomplish alone. Each of these roles demands wisdom and power from God. Each demands a willingness to suffer.

The mission that God has given you starts with who you are. God has called you as a specific person in a specific culture in a specific country in a specific place in time, and you are who you are because of all of those things. God's call involves living in Christ right there.

The mission that God has given you continues as you connect to others who also follow Christ. As a group you have an identity. You have a mission together, which you will find as you hear the mind of Christ. And you each have a role to play, for the sake of that mission.

I love that my denomination advocates abstinence from alcohol. I like that we provide a Christian community where an alcoholic will never be offered a drink. I like that wherever I go, whatever party I might attend, someone who needs to choose not to drink will never 'not drink' alone. That is a mission I can participate in, even though in some circles people are bound to look at me funny and think I'm holier-than-thou.

However, our church also has a biker ministry. People come to church on their motorcycles wearing helmets and leather, and they look a little different than I do. I have only ridden a motorcycle once in my life, and I was terrified. But those men and women love bikes; they love the people and the lifestyle, and they love Jesus. And they figure out how to reprioritize the biker culture in Christ. I could not do what they do, at least not well. But I am so glad that they do it.

My kids grew up in the video game age, and I have heard the debates over the effects of playing them. But one of my kids had what I think is a perfect example of an NVP Church idea. What if, he says, Christian gamers got together on some of these online role playing games and started a Bible study? What if your dwarf or elf or cyborg character established a league that met every week to talk about God? What would it look like to live in the online world in Christ?

How do we hear our call to mission? We find the answer as we live in Christ with one another. That has to involve more than worshipping together on Sunday mornings, as important as that is. We can only live

Christ's mission in the world in weakness and foolishness if we are first willing to live together that way.

Remember those bands of suffering Christians that I envied in chapter 1? I still want to be a part of that kind of community. I realize that all of those techniques that we use to form the identity of a group and to encourage people to conform to that identity, those are the very things I need to help me to live my own identity in Christ. He has given me his Spirit on the inside, but I also need his gift of others on the outside. I find models there of the behaviors that I want to imitate. I look at one or two people and I think, "Oh, I *like* the way Jesus looks in him. I want to live more like that." I sense, too, the expectations of the community, and although I have to evaluate them in light of God's Spirit in me, I can also use them to evaluate me in light of God's Spirit in them. The community of God's people helps me to live my own identity in Christ.

I have found five questions that are useful as I live this identity.[3] I have designed them to apply Paul's corrections in our cultural context. My accountability partner Kim and I answer them in emails to each other every week, sharing the ways that we fail and the ways we succeed.

1. *What was God's mission for you this week?* This question relates to both our group and our role identities. It invites us to think about the situations where God has called us. In each of those contexts, what role might God want you to play? How is the Holy Spirit leading you? Kim and I find that our answers to this question often stay the same from week to week. Many of our missions are long term: working in our churches, being present in difficult relationships. We also find unexpected short-term missions, sometimes as simple as listening to a friend. Once a week, we tell each other what we're doing.

2. *In what ways have you been able to cooperate with that mission?* Here is a chance to witness to the power of the Holy Spirit in our lives and give praise to God for what he is doing in and through us. The wording of the question assumes that we are cooperating with God, reinforcing that expectation. Sometimes I write to Kim about external missions, like the way God helped me faithfully finish the last few weeks of a project when I was tempted to cut corners. Sometimes I have written about internal missions, like when I listened to God's

3. These questions are listed by themselves at the end of the book so that you can copy them for use in small groups.

call to get my devotional life back on track. This question helps us share with each other the ways that God walks with us through the missions that he gives us and the way he supports us through any suffering that's involved.

3. *What has gotten in the way of you cooperating with that mission?* This is a more traditional accountability question. It's a good place to go through the ten commandments or any other list of possible sin areas to find those where God might want us to walk in a more holy way. Beyond specific sins, though, it's also a question that invites us to look at our cultural assumptions and find the ways that our traditions and habits might be keeping us from obeying God's call when they rise too high in our ladder of identity. In that sense, then, we may answer this question by talking about the suffering that obedience requires.

4. *What weakness or suffering have you offered to God this week?* This question reminds us of our dependence on our community and the sovereignty of God. It acknowledges that the outcome of God's plan does not depend on any one of us, but that by the grace of God we are who we are and we do what we do by the power of his Spirit at work in us (1 Cor 15:10). By offering our weaknesses and suffering to God, we acknowledge our need for God's wisdom, our need for God's power, and our need for help from the community of other followers of Christ.

5. *Who else have you noticed cooperating with God's plan for his or her life this week?* The last question leads naturally into this one. It helps us to value other faithful believers, other gifts, and other ministries. It requires us at least once a week to notice what God is doing through someone else. This other person is frequently someone who has gifts that are completely different from our own. By telling each other about these people, we remind ourselves that we are coworkers in God's field. We also may discover new models to follow.

So, how does this work? Well, you tell me. This book is all about the *I prayed, God said.* How is God asking you to adjust your life for his mission? What will he do if you say yes?

The Not-Very-Persecuted Church

Accountability Questions

1. What was God's mission for you this week?

2. In what ways have you been able to cooperate with that mission?

3. What has gotten in the way of you cooperating with that mission?

4. What weakness or suffering have you offered to God this week?

5. Who else have you noticed cooperating with God's plan for his or her life this week?

Bibliography

All translations of classical texts have been taken from the Loeb Classical Library (Cambridge: Harvard University Press) unless noted otherwise.

Andrew, J. L. Sherrill, et al. *God's Smuggler*. New York: New American Library, 1967.

Bock, D. L., and B. M. Fanning. *Interpreting the New Testament Text: Introduction to the Art and Science of Exegesis*. Wheaton: Crossway, 2006.

Boy Scouts of America. *Boy Scouts of America: The Official Handbook for Boys*. New York: Cosimo Classics, 2010.

Bruce, F. F. *The Book of the Acts*. Grand Rapids: Eerdmans, 1988.

Campbell, W. S. *Paul and the Creation of Christian Identity*. London; New York: T & T Clark, 2006.

Comby, J. *How to Read Church History*. New York: Crossroad, 1985.

Cymbala, J., and D. Merrill. *Fresh Wind, Fresh Fire: What Happens When God's Spirit Invades the Heart of His People*. Grand Rapids: Zondervan, 1997.

Dekker, J., and L. Neely. *Torches of Joy: The Dynamic Story of a Stone Age Tribe's Encounter with the Gospel of Jesus Christ*. Seattle: YWAM Publishing, 1993.

DeSilva, D. A. *New Testament Themes*. St. Louis: Chalice Press, 2001.

Dunn, J. D. G. *The Theology of Paul the Apostle*. Grand Rapids: Eerdmans, 1998.

Ehrensperger, K. *Paul and the Dynamics of Power: Communication and Interaction in the Early Christ-Movement*. London; New York: T & T Clark, 2007.

Ellemers, N., R. Spears, et al. "Self and Social Identity." *Annual Review of Psychology* 53, no. 1 (2002): 161–86.

Friesen, S. J. "Prospects for a Demography of the Pauline Mission: Corinth among the Churches." In *Urban Religion in Roman Corinth: Interdisciplinary Approaches*, edited by D. N. Schowalter and S. J. Friesen. Cambridge, MA: Harvard Divinity School, 2005.

Glancy, J. A. *Slavery in Early Christianity*. Oxford; New York: Oxford University Press, 2002.

Hogg, M. A., and D. Abrams. *Social Identifications: A Social Psychology of Intergroup Relations and Group Processes*. London; New York: Routledge, 1988.

Hybels, B., and M. Mittelberg. *Becoming a Contagious Christian*. Grand Rapids: Zondervan, 1994.

Jenkins, R. *Social Identity*. 2 ed. London; New York: Routledge, 2005.

Kearsley, R. A. "Women in Public Life in the Roman East: Iunia Theodora, Claudia Metrodora and Phoebe, Benefactress of Paul." *Tyndale Bulletin* 50, no. 2 (1999): 189–211.

Longenecker, B. W. "Exposing the Economic Middle: A Revised Economy Scale for the Study of Early Urban Christianity." *Journal for the Study of the New Testament* 31, no. 3 (2009): 243–78.

Marston, L. R. *From Age to Age a Living Witness: A Historical Interpretation of Free Methodism's First Century*. Winona Lake, IN: Light and Life Press, 1960.

Meeks, W. A. *The First Urban Christians: The Social World of the Apostle Paul*. New Haven: Yale University Press, 2003.

Murphy-O'Connor, J. *St. Paul's Corinth: Text and Archaeology*. Collegeville: Liturgical Press, 2002.

Shakespeare, W. and A. Durband. *Twelfth Night, or, What You Will*. Woodbury, N.Y.: Barron's, 1985.

Stearns, R. *The Hole in Our Gospel*. Nashville: Thomas Nelson, 2009.

Still, T. D., and D. G. Horrell. *After the First Urban Christians: The Social-Scientific Study of Pauline Christianity Twenty-Five Years Later*. London; New York: Continuum, 2010.

Tajfel, H. 1978. *Differentiation Between Social Groups: Studies in the Social Psychology of Intergroup Relations*, edited by J. Tajfel. European Monographs in Social Psychology 14. London: Published in cooperation with European Association of Experimental Social Psychology by Academic Press.

Theissen, G. *The Social Setting of Pauline Christianity: Essays on Corinth*. Philadelphia: Fortress Press, 1982.

Thiselton, A. C. *The First Epistle to the Corinthians: A Commentary on the Greek Text*. Grand Rapids: Eerdmans, 2000.

Tucker, J. B. "Baths, Baptism, and Patronage: The Continuing Role of Roman Social Identity in Corinth." In *Reading Paul in Context*, edited by K. Ehrensperger and J. B. Tucker. London: T. & T. Clark, 2010.

———. "Intercultural Interaction and Identity Formation in Pauline Tradition: The Continuation of Gentile Identity in Christ." Paper presented at the Society of Biblical Literature, Atlanta, November 20, 2010.

———. "The Role of Civic Identity on the Pauline Mission in Corinth." *Didaskalia* (*Otterburne, Man.*) 19, no. 1 (2008): 71–91.

———. *You Belong to Christ: Paul and the Formation of Social Identity in 1 Corinthians 1—4* Eugene, Or.: Pickwick Publications, 2010.

Turner, J. C. 1987. "A Self-categorization Theory." Pages 42–67 in *Rediscovering the Social Group: A Self-categorization Theory*, edited by J. C. Turner, et al. Oxford: Blackwell.

Warren, R. *The Purpose Driven Church: Growth without Compromising Your Message & Mission*. Grand Rapids: Zondervan, 1995.

White, J. L. *Light from Ancient Letters*. Philadelphia: Fortress Press, 1986.

Williams, C. "Abraham as a Figure of Memory in John 8.31–59." In *European Studies on Christian Origins*, edited by M. Goodacre, 205–22. London: T&T Clark, 2011.

Winter, B. W. *Roman Wives, Roman Widows: The Appearance of New Women and the Pauline Communities*. Grand Rapids: Eerdmans, 2003.

Witherington, B., III. *Making a Meal of It: Rethinking the Theology of the Lord's Supper*. Waco, TX: Baylor University Press, 2007.

Zetterholm, M. *Approaches to Paul: A Student's Guide to Recent Scholarship*. Minneapolis: Fortress Press, 2009.

www.ingramcontent.com/pod-product-compliance
Lightning Source LLC
Chambersburg PA
CBHW071944100426

42737CB00046BA/2263